A LITTLE OF ALL THESE

An Estonian Childhood

A LITTLE OF ALL THESE
An Estonian Childhood

Tania Alexander

To Anne —
with best wishes
Tania

June 1987

JONATHAN CAPE
THIRTY-TWO BEDFORD SQUARE
LONDON

First published 1987
Copyright © 1987 by Tania Alexander
Jonathan Cape Ltd, 32 Bedford Square, London WC1B 3EL

British Library Cataloguing in Publication Data

Alexander, Tania
A little of all these: an Estonian childhood.
1. Estonia—Social life and customs
I. Title
947'.41084'0924   DK511.E53

ISBN 0—224—02400—0

The author and publishers are grateful to the Estate of Meriel Buchanan for permission to reprint an extract from *Ambassador's Daughter* on pages 37–8.

Phototypeset by Wyvern Typesetting Ltd, Bristol
Printed in Great Britain by
Butler & Tanner Ltd,
Frome and London

To Bernard

For John, Natasha, Helen
and our grandchildren

Contents

Illustrations

FIGURES   *page*

Grateful acknowledgment is made to the Gorky Museum, Moscow, for permission to reproduce photographs of Maxim Gorky (nos 15 and 16). All other illustrations are taken from the author's personal archives.

Acknowledgments

As long ago as 1980 Rache Lovat Dickson, the author and publisher, persuaded me to embark on this memoir. I am deeply indebted to him for his encouragement and help with the first draft.

I also wish to thank George Robertson of the Canadian Broadcasting Corporation for his interest and advice in the early stages; my cousin Gerhardt von Benckendorff for providing me with a clear picture of my family's Baltic background; and Mary Young for her untiring involvement, which went far beyond her excellent typing.

Finally I must thank my son-in-law, Tim Suter. With great tact and sympathy he was able to draw out of me much that was vital to the book, and his editorial judgment enabled me to give a more coherent form to my story. Without his help and professional support I could not have achieved what I set out to do.

A LITTLE OF ALL THESE
An Estonian Childhood

Introduction

The Baltic philosopher Count Hermann Keyserling, whose famous travel diary was written in 1914, once remarked: 'I am not a Dane, not a German, not a Swede, not a Russian nor an Estonian, so what am I – a little of all these.'

I share his sense of confused identity. I was born in St Petersburg in Russia, but as a young child I was taken to Estonia, a province of Russia which was later to become the northernmost of the three independent Baltic States created in the aftermath of the First World War of 1914–18. The Estonians seized the opportunity afforded by the Russian Revolution in 1917 and the defeat of the German army by the Allies in 1918 to throw off the foreign domination of centuries and finally to achieve political independence in 1920. I grew up in that country, which survived for only twenty years between two World Wars. And yet, although I technically became an Estonian citizen, I have always felt myself to be more Russian than anything else. Russian was my first language. Both my parents were Russian citizens by birth: my father was of Baltic origin, my mother was a Russian from the Ukraine. The place where I was brought up, Kallijärv* in Estonia, was originally in Russia and despite the political changes in that part of the world remained always, for me, essentially Russian, and therefore had a very different atmosphere from other, perhaps more typically, Baltic homes.

My childhood was spent in a period of considerable unrest; and growing up in Estonia I saw at first hand what happens when the world polarises between two powerful political extremes and moderation is threatened, and finally destroyed. For the twenty years I lived there, Estonia was independent;

---

* pronounced Kaleeyairv

but I witnessed the destructive power of the régimes created by Hitler and Stalin, and the effect they had on a young democracy. I visited Russia before the Stalinist purges, and felt a natural sympathy for the people who I believed were trying to build a fairer world; but I also lived among people who had been robbed by the revolution of all they believed in. For centuries the Balts were the most powerful landlords in Estonia, as well as holding high positions in the service of the Tsar; and they were now, as a small racial minority, having to come to terms with their total powerlessness.

As I grew up I came to realise the full meaning of the political upheaval I had lived through, and as a result to respect the courage with which those closest to me had responded to the change and to the loss of all they had known. The First World War, the Russian Revolution and the Estonian War of Independence swept away their world, just as completely as the Second World War destroyed the world in which I was brought up.

Several characters, whose portraits appear in the book, stand out in their resistance to the anguish of personal loss and the hardships of that period. In particular, my early life was influenced by three women, all of them complex characters and strong personalities, who had to find their own way of adapting to very different lives from those they might have expected to enjoy. My Irish governess, Micky, sacrificed her family and suffered exile – a mother ostracised by the pressure of Victorian values. My Aunt Zoria lost everyone who was dear to her, as well as her homeland and her position in society. And my mother, who stayed behind in Russia throughout the terrifying events of the revolution and civil war, lost her home, her husband and, perhaps most important to her, her great love – a loss which profoundly affected the rest of her life. These three people are linked by one common feature: they were survivors, determined to hold on to what they had salvaged and achieved; forced by circumstances to become independent; showing great courage in forging new lives for themselves.

I responded to each of them in different ways. Micky I

always, quite simply, adored, and she in her turn lavished all her affection on me, and my brother and cousin, the other two children in her care. Aunt Zoria, by contrast, too preoccupied perhaps with her own much younger children, appeared to give nothing by way of warmth to us older children. We respected her, but the deep affection she inspired took longer to make itself felt. As for my mother, after her return to Estonia from Russia we felt that we meant a great deal to her, and when she was with us her warm personality drew us towards her. But we did not have the same intensity of feeling for her as we did for Micky, perhaps because she was so little with us as children, and because we very soon realised that we had to share her with other people.

I have also had the good fortune to be exposed to a number of other powerful personalities, and this book is therefore also a reflection of those people. As a child, I knew Maxim Gorky and spent one summer with him at his villa in Sorrento: a man of tremendous humanity and gentleness, as well as great strength of personality and conviction, who had a profound effect on my life and thinking. H.G. Wells, too, I knew well and came to admire. Despite his self-centredness and streak of vanity, he was always approachable; he never tried to overawe with his position or standing, but was quite natural with everyone.

The Second World War is as far as I take my own story in this book, for it forms a natural barrier. After I left Estonia I came to live with my mother in London, but I have written only briefly about this, for the book is about a different period and a different place. It is the memory of Kallijärv, my home for almost the first twenty years of my life, which has prompted me to write this book – the memory not only of the place which gave me the security and roots so essential for a happy childhood, but also of all the people who lived there and all those who came to stay. It was they who influenced my childhood and adolescence. They were my world, and the only world which I knew and loved until I came to England. It was destroyed by the Second World War and has gone for ever. It is that world which I have tried to describe for those who will never have lived through a revolution, and for whom Estonia is a far-distant land somewhere between Germany and Russia. I would like to think of this book as a tribute to the people who lived in Kallijärv and to the spirit which it embodied in the midst of those troubled times.

CHAPTER I
Prelude

In the spring of 1918, six months after the Bolshevik October Revolution, my brother and I, aged five and three, were taken for safety from our Petrograd* home to join our father who was already on his estate, Yendel, some fifty miles east of Reval (now Tallinn) in the Russian province of Estonia. But my first clear memory is of events a year later, when civil war was raging in Russia and the Estonians were fighting their own battles against both Russian and German domination.

As there had been pillaging by armed gangs at Yendel and in the neighbourhood, we had been temporarily moved to my grandmother's house, Kallijärv, by the lake a quarter of a mile away. On the morning of April 18th, 1919, my father had gone to see to things on the estate and at the Great House. He had told our Russian nurse, Mariussa, that he would be back in time for lunch. At first he had suggested taking 'his little woman', as he used to call me, with him, but Mariussa had refused to let me go and had put me back in the cot. I can remember him standing beside me while I raged at her for not letting me go with him.

At one o'clock he had not yet returned and my brother Paul, cousin Kira, Mariussa and I set out to meet him. We walked along the edge of the lake, prodding the floating ice with sticks. The lake had been frozen all winter but now the ice was melting rapidly. As we turned the second corner we saw in front of us the body of a man lying across the path. Mariussa screamed and tried to raise the body, but it was too late. She then hurriedly ushered us away, but we had already seen that the man was our father and that he was dead. I don't think that any of us cried or even quite understood; but I can well

* St Petersburg was renamed Petrograd in 1914

remember being aware that something very terrible had happened.

My next memory is of white sheets over our large dining-table on the summer veranda, and my father lying there with only his waxlike face showing, surrounded by a mountain of flowers, sheets and candles. An apparently endless stream of aunts and relatives came and wept, and a constant flow of villagers and people from the estate arrived with bunches of flowers. We children would go into the room, sensing rather than understanding their grief and the tragedy that had befallen us all. This lasted for several days until the body was moved to the Great House. From there began the funeral procession. We watched from the steps of the house as our father's coffin was carried on the shoulders of his brothers along the long avenue. At the end of this a carriage took the coffin, and mourners followed to the family vault five miles away. The eldest of four brothers, he was only thirty-six when he died.

It was never clearly established who had fired the shots which killed my father. People said later that they had heard three shots, and our Irish governess Micky, who had also heard them, had had a premonition that at that moment something had happened to him.

My father, Ioann von Benckendorff, was of Baltic origin. The Benckendorffs were members of the Baltic nobility who had come to that part of the world in the fourteenth century. My father himself was a career diplomat serving at the outbreak of the First World War in the Imperial Russian Embassy in Berlin. Among his family and friends he was always known as John, spelled Djon.

In 1911 he had married my mother, Maria (known as Moura) Ignatievna Zakrevsky, sister of his friend and colleague at the embassy, Platon Zakrevsky. At the outbreak of war three years later he was immediately recalled from Berlin to the Ministry of Foreign Affairs in St Petersburg. Before long he volunteered for military service and was appointed to the staff of the Headquarters of the Northern Russian Army. But the disintegration of the Russian army in 1917 and the abdication of the Tsar affected my father deeply. Disillusioned by the collapse of the world and the society in which he had been brought up, he returned to his estate in Estonia, while my mother remained behind in Petrograd.

The country was in a state of chaos and lawlessness; atrocities and murders were a daily occurrence. Like all landowners at the time, my father had been receiving threatening anonymous letters. But he was a fearless man. A loyal subject of the Tsar, his crime was that he belonged to a class which for generations had inherited and owned the land under a system which prevented the advancement of the local population. But he firmly believed that he and his family had been good to the people on the estate, and I have often been told by the peasants and villagers that he always treated every man fairly and kindly. Although he had served as a Staff Officer in the war, after the collapse of the Russian army he welcomed the German military presence in Estonia – a subject of bitter disagreement with my mother – on the grounds that it would stop Bolshevism spreading and restore order to the country. This was a view held by most of the Baltic landlords.

Several years after his death, when I was about eight years old, I had to walk along the same path to piano lessons given by a woman who lived near Yendel, the Great House which had been our family home. After the establishment of Estonia's independence in 1920 and the expropriation of the landowners, it had become a state agricultural college.

It was a secluded and beautiful walk, which took you along a lane and then up a steep hill. At the top of this hill you turned left till you came to a bridge, which joined this hill to yet another. The trees became thicker and the road darker as you neared the bridge. The Devil's Bridge it was called. It was on the path just below this bridge that we had found my father's body. My heart beat faster as I began to cross the bridge. How exactly had it happened? Had the assassin stood on the bridge waiting for him to pass, and then fired? With my mind filled with pictures of the time I had found his body, I steeled myself to look down at the spot where he had been murdered. Where his body had lain was a bunch of fresh flowers, left there on the anniversary of his death. Right up to the time when I was quite grown up I remember anonymous little bunches of flowers placed there every year.

I now had to turn and cross the rest of the bridge, but I knew that a few paces more and there would be a large clearing; it would no longer be dark and eerie, and all the terror and awe of the previous hundred yards would leave me.

But even today, whenever I come across a small overhead bridge, that strange feeling of awe and fear momentarily returns.

CHAPTER II
Early Years in Estonia

When we children were hustled out of Petrograd in what must have been the most exciting and dangerous journey I ever made, we were sent off in a postal coach with Micky, who had been fitted out with a false passport and told not to say a word. To be heard speaking English could well have been fatal, as Great Britain was at war with Germany, and the German army was still occupying the former Russian province of Estonia. Travelling with us was a Swiss escort who was experienced in taking people across borders. We also had with us our grandmother's two fox terriers which we children had been told to try to keep under control. Each one of us had been provided with a shoulder bag containing sandwiches for the long day's journey, and something to give the dogs. Progress was slow as there was still some unmelted snow on the ground.

Although there were frontier guards of whom we were naturally frightened, there was no actual defined frontier; and it was not until we finally arrived at Yendel, where my father was waiting for us, that we knew we were safe at last.

We arrived in Estonia at a crucial time in the country's struggle for independence. As well as resisting any attempts at Bolshevik penetration, the Estonians knew that they would eventually have to fight against German expansionism. Kerensky, as head of the Provisional Government, had taken the first step in agreeing to their autonomy in a federal state and establishing an Estonian National Council under Jaan Poska, the nationalist leader. But it soon became clear that Estonian independence would be threatened by Germany as long as Russia remained in the war. By September 1917 the Germans had occupied Riga and the Estonian islands. The Bolshevik Revolution on November 7th, 1917 brought renewed hopes of peace for the Estonians; but it was greeted in

Reval by the establishment of a soviet which declared itself the legal government and opened the door to Bolshevik troops from other parts of Russia to resist the continuing advance of the Germans.

There were two options open to the Estonians to save themselves from Bolshevik domination. One was to appeal to the Allied powers for recognition, the other was to appeal to the Germans. While the Estonian National Council made approaches to the Allies through the British Ambassador in Stockholm, the Balts of Latvia, Lithuania and Estonia made a formal appeal to the German Government asking the Kaiser to take the provinces under his protection. The Baltic barons themselves were by no means sympathetic to the German dream of the *Drang nach Osten*, and did not wish to see their countries becoming part of the German Reich; but they felt that the German army was the force most likely to ward off what they believed to be the greater threat of Bolshevik rule. They therefore requested the German army to occupy the rest of Estonia and advance as far as possible to the east at the expense of the Soviets. The Germans responded to this appeal and the Bolsheviks abandoned Reval on February 23rd, 1918. This was the signal for the Estonian National Council to repeat its proclamation of the Estonian Republic, but the Germans took little notice. After several weeks of negotiations, the Bolsheviks, much to the distress of the western Allies, agreed to sign the Treaty of Brest-Litovsk (March 1918) which ended the war between Germany and Russia, at the same time declaring that the Baltic States would no longer be under Russian sovereignty. In the treaty Russia formally renounced all rights to interfere in the internal affairs of those countries.

It was at this time, the spring of 1918, that we were brought from Russia into Estonia. Although the Bolsheviks were no longer in the country and the Germans had fully occupied it, there was still great unrest and it was clear that there would be further fighting. In fact, German control of the Baltic States lasted only until November of that year: with the defeat of their armies in the west and the signing of the armistice on

November 11th, the German armies in the east retreated to Riga, evacuating Estonia completely.

The retreat of the Germans was followed by the period of greatest lawlessness in Estonia, which was laid open to its second Bolshevik invasion within a year, and which took the Red Army to within twenty miles of Reval by the end of November. The country was in a state of turmoil, with armed groups moving about plundering the estates and stealing horses and cows. Kind peasants would often come to Yendel and give us advance warning that this or that group was in the neighbourhood. We would then be bundled into the stables or hidden in the garden till they had gone. They would come into the house, slash pictures, throw excreta on the walls and take away whatever they could.

It is hardly surprising that the events we were witnessing should affect us as children, but it is also true that we were too young to realise their seriousness, and we treated them more as a game. Our nursery quarters were on the top floor. One day we were not to be found and Mariussa ran downstairs to look for us. She found us under the huge dining-room table. 'Don't come too close,' said my five-year-old brother, 'we are playing Bolsheviks.'

The country was now plunged into a bloody war of liberation. There was little help to be had for the Estonians from the Allied powers, but at the end of 1918 a national uprising took place and succeeded in driving the Bolsheviks from the land. In the middle of this war, I can still remember times of apparent peacefulness at Yendel. I can see our nursery and a very long corridor along which my brother and I used to play catch. I remember our stocky coachman, Konoshenko, bringing the coach and horses to the door to take Micky and us children for a drive.

Early in 1919 the Bolshevik forces retreated from Estonia. There was, however, still a German threat in the south where a force under General von der Golz had been fighting the Bolsheviks, aided by White Russian troops and the newly created Baltic *Landeswehr*, recruited entirely from the Baltic aristocracy. Although the western Allies were at first happy to

see a German force fighting the Bolsheviks, they were slow to
realise the danger of a restoration of German ambitions in the
east. The Estonians were determined to thwart the plans of
General von der Golz and the Baltic barons, and in June 1919
they halted the German advance. On June 20th the Treaty of
Versailles was signed, which stipulated that all German troops
should immediately evacuate the Baltic lands. The last German troops were out of Estonia by the end of the year and the
Landeswehr, limited to 2,000 men, was placed under the
command of Colonel Alexander – General Alexander of the
Second World War – to resist any further attempts at Bolshevik penetration. In 1920 a peace treaty was signed between
Estonia and Soviet Russia by which Russia recognised the
independence of the state of Estonia 'for all time'. Estonia was
at last independent of, and at peace with, her powerful
neighbour; the other great powers followed with recognition
and in 1921 Estonia was admitted to the League of Nations.
During their independence, the Estonians under President
Konstantin Päts did great things for their people, but their
hard-won independence lasted only twenty years until 1940,
when Estonia became one of the pawns of the Second World
War and was finally reabsorbed into the USSR.

In their measures of land reform the Estonian Government
allowed the Baltic landlords to retain five per cent of the land
they had owned, giving the children of landlords killed in
the revolution, or the war, a home and the equivalent of a
smallholding on their father's former estate. But in early 1919,
when Estonia first freed itself from foreign rule, the people
took immediate revenge upon their former lords and masters.
Our lives at Yendel were shattered one day when, our father
being away in town, a gang of men got into the living rooms,
plundering and destroying and stealing, leaving the Great
House in a terrible mess. It was decided to move us to Kallijärv
on the lake, where my paternal grandmother had lived, and
where we would be safe until order was restored. Within a
month of our moving, however, my father was murdered; and
we were left at Kallijärv in the care of our nanny, Mariussa,
our governess Micky and a succession of aunts or, rather,

remote relations whom we called aunts. Shortly after this the Great House and the estate – together with all the estates in Estonia – were confiscated. Later, under the provisions of the new Estonian government, my brother and I were given Kallijärv in joint ownership; and this was the place where we were brought up and which we so dearly loved.

Kallijärv had originally been the summer residence of my widowed grandmother. The house stood on its own by a small lake in a large clearing in the forest. It was a low building made entirely of wood with a large veranda, which during the summer months became the centrepiece of our lives. Behind the veranda there was a drawing-room, which was rarely used in the summer but in the winter months became the living-room for our family. The bedrooms, which were of a modest size and simply furnished, all led off a long, dark corridor at the end of which there was a large kitchen.

Here we lived, summer and winter, until I was eleven, isolated from the rest of the world, relying on our own amusements and resources. It provided a simple background which allowed us a free and self-sufficient existence. For affection we had Micky, whom we loved and who loved us; we had each other (my brother, Paul; my cousin, Kira, and our Benckendorff cousin, Goga, who was my age exactly; and later his two much younger little half-sisters, Alexandra and Nathalie) to play with. Paul was only just over a year older than me. We were and have remained devoted, but as a small child he was less lively, and more withdrawn, than the rest of us. We rarely quarrelled, but if we did it was I who was the more hot-tempered. I think that an almost entirely matriarchal household was hardly the best atmosphere for a boy who was growing up. We also had Roosi who came daily from the village to help Leeni, our general factotum. By working twelve hours a day Leeni somehow managed to do all the cooking, bread-making and much more still. She worked harder than anyone I have ever met and never complained. When the Second World War broke out (she must have been in her sixties), she wrote to me in England to say that her feet were so bad she felt it was time to give up work and get married.

In winter we had few visitors. It was bitterly cold, the lake was frozen and snow lay five or six feet deep from December to April. We had primitive home-made sledges and skis but we only learned to ski on the flat. The house was kept warm by tiled stoves, which burned peat and usually extended into two rooms, heating both. We had no electricity in those days, but there were paraffin lamps for every room. These were lined up on a table in an ante-room outside the kitchen every morning; the wicks were then cleaned and the lamps were filled with paraffin ready to be picked up by us in the evening as we went to bed. The sitting-room was lined with pictures of rather forbidding-looking Benckendorff ancestors, including a portrait of Christopher Benckendorff, the first member of the family to settle in Estonia in the fourteenth century, and from whom we and all branches of Benckendorffs descended. The windows had shutters and very few of them had curtains. The bedroom floors were bare uncovered boards and there were no ornaments or bits and pieces about. The dining-room was dark with a huge table in the middle, while the walls were lined with bookshelves covered with glass doors.

As a child I thought, of course, that Kallijärv was exactly what a house should be like. Thinking about it now, I realise that there were few objects of beauty in the house. But we were indifferent to possessions and grew up to believe that, as long as there was a bed to sleep on, it was almost bad taste to think of material things. In fact, I suppose since everything had once been lost in the revolution, there was no point, it was felt, in acquiring new possessions even if there had been sufficient money to buy them. There was nothing of bad taste about, but also nothing decorative or valuable. Our family, and all those who had suffered a similar fate, had a strange kind of pride and a sense of superiority about being 'above' such things. For them money was all right when it was in the hands of those who knew how to use it (meaning themselves) – otherwise it was vulgar. On the other hand, we were encouraged to respond to the beauty of landscapes, trees and flowers. In Kallijärv it was the place itself and the surroundings which we loved.

In the years immediately after the revolution, and in the early 1920s, there was enough to eat, but there was little variety in our diet. Our small farm provided corn and eggs, but meat was always very scarce. Sometimes for dinner there would be only a large dish of vegetables and gravy, with home-made black bread and butter, baked in a large bread oven. At tea-time there was always a huge bowl of sour milk standing in the larder, from which we could help ourselves. A great treat was when each of us was allowed to beat up an egg with sugar; this we called 'goggle-moggle'. It had its own ritual: each one of us would beat up his or her yolk in an individual cup; all the whites were pooled and subjected to a lot of beating; then a little of the beaten white was added to each yolk with sugar. When all this had been done we would then sit down and relish the weekly treat. In later years, when we were taking our school exams and working late, we would strengthen ourselves with one of these concoctions and teach our friends how to make it. I have since even passed it on to my own children.

Goggle-moggle was our only culinary achievement. We still expected, and were brought up to expect, that meals were served without any effort on the part of any member of the family. None of the aunts who looked after us ever learned even to boil an egg.

From early childhood we spoke Russian, German and English at home, and learned both to read and to write in those languages. At that time Estonian was still a developing language. We spoke it mostly with villagers and servants. We learned by ear to speak it fluently, but never to write it.

I can remember – I must have been about four – a large Russian children's book with charming old-fashioned illustrations, a kind of A B C. There was also a very handsome volume of Wilhelm Bush, the German humorist – *Struwelpeter*. This was another favourite. The cover, with a large dishevelled boy whose fingernails had grown into long claws because he was naughty and would never have them cut, is one of the most abiding memories of my early reading. Later among my first English books I remember a copy of *Little Lord Fauntleroy* in a green and gold binding with rather nauseating pictures. The contrast of their saccharine sentimentality with the gruesome Germanic morality was rather striking, and although I am now horrified by *Struwelpeter*, I know that at the time I preferred its ghoulishness. Later there were the 'Katie' books and my favourite Hans Andersen fairy tale 'The Snow Queen'. They must all have been part of a haphazard collection of books which had been rescued from the Great House before it was confiscated.

For the whole of our early life we were, in effect, without parents. Our father was dead and our mother, we had been told, had stayed in Petrograd with her own mother, who was ill. In fact my grandmother died in April 1919, only a week or two after my father, though I don't think we heard about her death until much later. We knew too that it was by then not easy to cross the border from Russia into Estonia, and Moura would have had difficulty even if she had wanted to join us.

During the next few years the grown-ups around us never mentioned Moura, nor did they know whether she would ever be coming back to us. All kinds of rumours had reached them from Moscow, but we knew nothing of all this at the time. Secrets were very carefully kept from children in those days, and a child does not question events or even want to think about things which might threaten its security. Micky did all she could to shelter us from the troubles and rumours around us. But my grandmother's old cook and his wife, who lived in a wing of the house, used to bring blood-curdling tales which we children overheard. There were stories of shootings and destruction. I remember hearing that a woman had been found hanged by her long hair in the woods near us. That image used to scare me for a long time. And Mariussa did not help with her stories of bogey-men coming to fetch us. The bogey-man she threatened us with was a deaf and dumb man from the village who was totally harmless, but we were terrified of him, entirely due to her threats. I remember her as a short, brisk little woman, her hair rigidly stretched back into a tight bun: as our nanny, she should have been the person to whom we were closest, but she encouraged no love from us and gave little in return. The ideal that instilling fear in a child could have any effect other than inspiring obedience never crossed her mind. Before long she left us to get married to a Pole. We didn't know him, but, with our ingrained Russian suspicion of Poles, we thought it no more than she deserved. I don't think we were very sorry when she left. Anyway, we still had our beloved Micky.

We had another great ally in the household and that was Roosi, our Estonian cook. She was a great friend to us children for many years. The complete opposite of Mariussa, she was earthy, spontaneous and generous. She had an intuitive sense of fun which endeared her to us, but she was also very sensible; she would always tell us when to stop. She had great native intelligence and plenty of common sense. From her we learned the facts of life, from her we 'borrowed' pennies to buy sweets; she was the one who sensibly answered our questions when other grown-ups were evasive or shut us up. When later she got married, she still came daily to work from the nearby village.

Roosi was the last person of our household who was still alive after the Second World War in the Soviet Republic of Estonia. She wrote regularly to me in England in childlike Estonian, giving news of herself and Kallijärv, till she died in 1970. She had found it difficult to adapt to a very different way of life under Soviet rule, but her children had done well; they had travelled all over the Soviet Union and their education and horizons were wider than they probably would have been under the old régime. But she wrote that she personally longed for the 'good old days', and always hoped to see us again. In the 1950s, having reached pensionable age, she wrote to ask my mother to send her a written testimonial of good character and work to cover the years 'spent in service of gentlefolk, so that I can prove to the Estonian Soviet authorities the number of my working years'. It seemed to us paradoxical that, in assessing the amount of the pension due to her, the Estonian Soviet authorities had to rely on a testimonial from a member of the despised ruling class.

Despite the chaos that surrounded us, these were times of almost carefree happiness. Micky and Roosi were strict, but their love and care for us meant that our childhood was as happy as, in the circumstances, it could be. It was not to last: in 1920 a great-aunt arrived to bring order to our household. As a former headmistress, it was a task to which she warmed. Constanza Edle von Rennenkampff, Aunt Cossé as we called her, was a disciplinarian. A spinster in her late fifties, she was aggressively proud of her aristocratic Baltic origins. An upright, corpulent figure, her grey hair taken up in a bun, she took everybody in hand. She was capable, efficient and very bossy and she provided a head of house which we were lacking. She was to teach us all the basic school subjects. To us children who had never been near a school in our lives, and who had never encountered any discipline other than that of Mariussa and Micky, Aunt Cossé was a severe shock and at the time we thought her terribly strict and rather mean.

Since the civil war food had always been scarce; but after Aunt Cossé's arrival it seemed to get scarcer and more monotonous. I can remember struggling with dishes of thin gruel with lumps of fat floating on the surface. We were convinced that Aunt Cossé was directly responsible for this deterioration; and we were also sure that she was feeding herself secretly at night. We even used to spy on her when we heard her going to the larder late in the evening, returning with biscuits that we would have loved to eat, but we were too scared of her to do anything about it. We also thought her absurdly pompous when she made Kira and me go up and curtsy to her, and kiss her hand after every meal and thank her, something I had never had to do before; and unkind when she made us copy out ten lines beginning with 'I must not ...' for any crime, no matter how small – even for a childish squabble between brother and sister.

There was one particular punishment Micky especially disliked, and with good reason. Whenever any of us had particularly displeased Aunt Cossé, she would write out our misdemeanour on a slip of cardboard – 'Must do her homework' or 'Must not be untruthful' – and during lunch and for the rest of the day the culprit was compelled to walk around with this warning dangling from his or her neck. Strangely, I do not remember minding this too much in itself, probably because there was, after all, nobody except ourselves to see it. What we did mind was the fear that there would be a row between Micky and Aunt Cossé, for Micky's indignation at her behaviour was great. Our chief worry was how to keep Micky from exploding.

Micky regarded Aunt Cossé as an intruder and was always attempting to undermine her authority. 'You don't have to thank her,' she would say under her breath to us. 'It's not her food. This is your house.' At meal-times Aunt Cossé sat at the head of the table. Micky was at the other end, next to the samovar which stood on a small table beside her, and emanating disapproval of almost everything Aunt Cossé did, from the meals she had ordered to the punishments she meted out.

This was my view of Aunt Cossé at the time. But I can see now that she deserved our sympathy more than our childish hatred, and in fact we really did respect her. First and foremost, she was a good teacher and gave all of us an excellent grounding in subjects we would not otherwise have known. There was virtually no ready money and she ran the household as best she could. It cannot have been easy for her and Micky's attitude was not exactly helpful.

Aunt Cossé endured life at Kallijärv for nearly five years, and her careful teaching paid off when in 1925 my father's family decided it was high time that we children went away to school. They settled on the German Gymnasium in the town of Wesenberg, which was coeducational and had a headmaster with the highest reputation. Aunt Cossé could now take up the task of running a finishing school, where her style of authority was better understood. She was, in truth, an organiser, and much happier when not teaching young children. Aunt Cossé's place was taken by Aunt Zoria, the Russian wife of my father's brother, Uncle Sasha. But still it was Micky who came first in our affections and our loyalties.

CHAPTER III
Micky

In our childhood, with so many comings and goings, so many rumours and so much change, the single important fixed point was Micky, our Irish governess who gave us constant affection and the security we lacked.

Micky's proper name was Margaret Wilson. She was to spend fifty-six years of her life in our family bringing up two generations.

In no sense was she the usual type of nanny or governess. Really she was neither. By the time of the Russian Revolution she had already spent twenty-five years on my grandfather's estate in the Ukraine, where as the governess she had always had servants to wait on her. As a result, she had no idea at all how to run a house. Instead, she had devoted herself to the bringing up of my mother's generation of the Zakrevskys and had lovingly cared for the children.

Her early life, like so much in my childhood, was shrouded in rumour and mystery, and it was not for many years that I was to discover the truth about her.

All we knew, or rather the story we had been told as we grew up, was that she was born in Liverpool, and had married an Irishman by whom she had a son and – as we believed – a daughter. When her husband left her and soon afterwards died in an Irish uprising, she had to support her children and was desperate to find employment. Relations took the children into their home while Micky provided money for their keep.

It was about that time – 1892 – that my grandfather, Ignatiy Platonovich Zakrevsky, came to England on a semi-official visit – where he met Sir Charles Dilke – and to Ireland, where among others he met Maud Gonne. Maud Gonne, the great love of W.B. Yeats and inspiration of many of his best poems, was a noted beauty who became a legendary figure in

Irish politics. Her father, Colonel Thomas Gonne, was a militant supporter of Home Rule. He had died when Maud was not yet twenty-one.

When my grandfather met Maud Gonne he mentioned to her that he would like to take a governess back to Russia with him to teach his seven-year-old twin daughters English. It was the fashion in Russia at that time to learn English and copy the English way of life – until then it had usually been French. Maud Gonne at once introduced my grandfather to Margaret Wilson, who she said had been her companion, and who was at present badly in need of a change, as her husband had recently died. She, Maud Gonne, persuaded Margaret Wilson to take the opportunity, and promised to have her baby girl well looked after while she was in Russia. A few weeks later my grandfather set out on his return journey to Russia, accompanied by Margaret Wilson, who had agreed to teach his children English for a year. But when the year was up, Margaret Wilson had become a devoted member of the family. She had become Ducky to all his children, including my mother, who was born the year after she arrived. Twenty years later she was still in Russia – ready to take on yet another generation; but she had become Micky to me, my brother and my cousin. One of us must have preferred 'Micky' to 'Ducky'.

We all knew that Micky was Mrs Margaret Wilson, that she had a daughter called Eileen whose married name was Mac-Bride, and from whom an occasional letter would arrive postmarked County Mayo in Ireland. We knew too that whenever this happened Micky would almost certainly be irritable and crotchety for the rest of the day. I suppose that we wondered at first what the mystery of her leaving her own family had been, but we soon learned not to ask questions. 'Run along. That's all long ago,' Micky would say.

When Margaret Wilson had arrived in Russia, she was a woman in her late twenties, tall, very good-looking and with a great deal of poise. She dressed simply, but with care. She wore a long dress to her ankles then and continued to do so to the end of her days. She was plunged into a wealthy household full of servants, nannies, wet-nurses, temporary governesses and tutors. Her first charges were my Uncle Bobik, then twelve years old, and my twin aunts, Assia and Alla, aged seven. When my mother was born and the attention of everyone was focused on the new arrival, Ducky too centred her affection on Moura. They lived on my grandfather's estate, Beriozovaya Rudka, in the Ukraine. Here Wilson – as my grandmother, who tried to keep everyone in their place, insisted on calling her – held a rather special place in the family. She gradually adopted the Zakrevsky family as her own, and commanded her own special position. She was not well educated, either in books or in household accomplishments. In fact, she hardly read at all and she could barely manage to write a letter. When I was a child, she still received *Woman's Weekly* regularly, but I suspect that she only turned the pages and read the headlines. She was not clever, but she was wise and intuitive.

After we moved to my father's estate in Estonia, she had to adapt to many hardships and a simpler life, for our sake. By that time she had become the mainstay and indispensable member of the family, lavishing affection on all three of us. She was quite strict. 'I want a new dress, Micky,' I would say. 'Then want shall be your master,' was Micky's tart reply. She taught us to sing 'Britons never, never, never shall be slaves ... ' in the heart of Estonia and we were roused by her patriotic feelings. She made everyone in the family speak English and in fifty years learned to speak only a few words of Russian. She was often moody in later years, but we knew how to humour her out of such moods. Nevertheless, her approval and disapproval somehow affected the whole household. As children, we sensed that there were areas of unhappiness somewhere in her life, but we didn't really know what they were. We knew only that she was always there, always on our side, ready to defend us. She was reserved, and together with an affectionate, gentle manner there was a surprising streak of rebelliousness in her character. This was largely demonstrated by her dislike of any exercise of authority, especially over us. Aunt Zoria, who replaced Aunt Cossé as head of the household, and whom we had to obey, Micky would dismiss as 'that Lady Macbeth – you don't have to listen to *her*'. She protected us and yet, in a curious way, I always felt that we too had to protect her from those who didn't understand her as we did, because we loved her dearly. She never spoke against religion, but she somehow conveyed to me that she regarded too much reliance on God with suspicion. She was unsentimental and totally self-contained. Everyone respected and took account of Micky. She had standards, definite standards which she inculcated into us without being able to express them. She approved or disapproved of things and people without much explanation, but we always knew what and whom she liked or didn't like. In our time she had no actual wages; but she always had a little money by her which she kept in a blue cloth bag in her bedroom. She never spent any money on herself. Everything she had was bought for her at her request, either by my mother when she later came on her biannual visits from abroad or, when we had grown up, by us.

She had come to the Zakrevskys in Russia and a Zakrevsky, in her eyes, could do no wrong. Although she had learned to love my father and to accept him as head of the family, she had little use for our Baltic aunts and relatives. Uncle Sasha, Aunt Zoria, as well as Aunt Cossé, she always regarded as intruders who had no right to what she considered belonged to 'Mary and her children'. To emphasise this she had armed herself with a toy rubber printing press into which she had fitted the rubber letters to spell my name, and would stamp books, sheets, towels and anything else she fancied, so that I should one day have them for my dowry. Years later (when I was married in London during the Second World War), my husband would dine out on the story that I had brought him as a dowry the promise of thirty-nine Russian fine linen sheets which were still waiting for me in Estonia.

When I left Estonia at the age of nineteen to come to England, I was heartbroken to have to leave Micky. She and I had been particularly close in recent years, because I was the last of her charges to leave home. During my final three years at school, she and I were paying guests in term-time in the town house of yet another Baltic aunt, Baroness Lotte Dellingshausen. We had a two-room flat across the courtyard, but had all our meals with Aunt Lotte and her family except for breakfast, which Micky prepared before sending me off to the coeducational day school I attended. If ever I might complain of a headache, Micky administered something called 'green powder' mixed into black coffee, to 'get your bowels moving, my dear'. I was unable to drink black coffee for years afterwards, remembering this sickly potion.

Micky always welcomed my school-friends; she preferred boys to girls and spoke English to them which they could hardly understand. Gradually as I grew older there were all sorts of school activities, and sometimes dances to go to. Boy-girl relationships at our age were pretty innocent in those days, but we were all 'in love' at various times. I remember one occasion when the boys' boarding-house of our school was giving a dance on a Friday evening. We were very much looking forward to this. Dances were usually over by eleven o'clock, and Micky always waited up for me to return. The young man who had invited you was in honour bound to walk you home. That evening Karen, a good friend of mine, had suggested that several of us go back to her house after the dance, and continue dancing to the gramophone there. Her parents were away and her older sister was in charge and would be amenable. We felt very daring and that made it all the more fun. At 12.30 a.m. we finally dispersed and the boys walked their respective girl friends back through the empty streets. As Peter and I turned the corner near my house, there was the imposing figure of an irate Micky in a vivid purple dressing-gown bearing down on us. To me this was a reassuring sight, however bizarre; to Peter she must have appeared terrifying. Characteristically her first thought was for me, but having established that I was all right she turned and glanced at Peter. 'Young man,' she said, 'you ought to be ashamed of yourself.' That was enough. Peter, utterly crushed, crept away and I followed Micky home. She treated me at first as if I had been through some terrible ordeal, then she made me drink hot cocoa and tucked me up in bed. 'We had a wonderful time, darling,' I said and kissed her goodnight. Micky smiled. 'I don't think Lady Macbeth would be very pleased,' she replied, 'but we won't tell her.'

Only a few years ago, I was staying with a friend for the weekend, when I noticed Maud Gonne MacBride's memoirs, *A Servant of the Queen*, on her shelves, and asked to take the book to bed with me. As I read I came across a passage where Maud Gonne was remembering a scene with her uncle shortly after her father's death:

> ... As I opened the drawing-room door, I heard Uncle William's voice, very hard and precise, saying: 'I tell you, my good woman, I don't believe you. That letter is no proof that the child was his.' A young woman in black was sitting in a chair; she was crying...
> 'Please go at once,' he continued addressing the young woman. 'Can't you see how improper your presence is here?'
> 'Oh! Miss Gonne, won't *you* help me?'
> 'If I can,' I said quietly, going over to her. 'Are you Mrs Robbins?'
> ... She was astonished when I said her name.

Maud Gonne, it seems, had addressed an envelope for her father to a Mrs Eleanor Robbins on the day before he died, and had also written a cheque in her favour for him as he was too weak to do it himself. At Mrs Robbins's mention of a baby, Maud Gonne began to see the truth, to her uncle's dismay:

> 'Where is the baby?' I whispered. She looked at me in a curious frightened and half-hostile way.
> 'She is safe, no one shall take her from me.' ...
> 'What is her name?'
> 'Daphne. I wouldn't come here at all, but I have no money and I don't know what to do. I am not one who tells lies. I want nothing from you but enough to keep the child till I can get work. I reared my son myself when my husband deserted us. My son is at sea now; but I have been ill and I can't get work and I can't let the child starve. The Colonel was good; he would never have left us unprovided.'

'How old is Daphne?' I asked.

'Six weeks. The Colonel never saw her. He was dead when I came out of hospital.'

'Please, Uncle, give her money at once! Can't you see she is desperate?' I said. 'We can't let her go like that; Tommy would wish us to help her.'

It ended by Uncle William handing out five sovereigns and promising to call on her.

I told her not to worry. Later I helped her to get a post to teach English in a Russian family, by saying she had been my companion.

Russians even under the old Czarist régime treated governesses as human beings. She grew as fond of those children as if they had been her own, and they loved her.

Could 'Mrs Robbins' have been our Micky? I was sure that here was some connection and I had to find out. I knew that Victor Gollancz was about to publish a biography of Maud Gonne and I contacted the author, Nancy Cardozo, who was still working on the book. She replied at once and confirmed my suspicions: Maud Gonne, with confusing discretion, had used fictitious names in her autobiography to hide the identity of her illegitimate half-sister. It was clear that 'Mrs Robbins' was really Margaret Wilson, our Micky! And 'Daphne' was really Eileen, Micky's daughter by Sir Thomas Gonne, Maud Gonne's father. Maud Gonne was prepared to help Eileen, but Micky had to be banished to avoid a scandal. My grandfather's visit from Russia produced the opportunity, and since she had no money and her own husband had abandoned her, she had no choice but to let her child be brought up by the family of her lover. Victimised as she was in a world of Victorian deception and cover-up, cruelty was better than an open scandal. She now had to leave her child behind for ever and make a life elsewhere. It must have needed great courage. But she had at least the certainty of Maud's loving interest in her half-sister. From then on Maud took care of the little girl, who was never to know her mother. After all these years I had the truth. I was stunned and saddened. I only hope that the love and devotion that we gave to Micky brought her happiness and peace: that might be some recompense for the sadness of her early life, and some return for the love and care that she showed us.

I came to understand Micky much better when I knew the truth of her story. I had accepted without question her position in the family and had taken for granted the loyalty she had always shown us; although I knew there were some things in her past she would not talk about, I had not realised the extent of the personal loss and anguish that she had suffered. Her lack of sentimentality had been learned the hardest way; in order to maintain Sir Thomas Gonne's reputation, she had been deprived of her child, even of her home; she had had to learn to adapt herself to completely new and alien conditions in a country she did not know and a language she did not understand. It was not surprising that she was so self-contained.

I also understood much better the rebellious side of Micky's character. The instinct of self-preservation and survival had made her quick to fight for her own rights and not prepared to submit tamely to any further imposition. She always stood up for those in her care, against treatment that she thought harsh or unjustified. Aunt Cossé, with her strict code of behaviour towards us, aroused in Micky a defensiveness that I had always appreciated but never understood; and I came to see more clearly why Micky had resented the intrusion of others into the care of us children.

I had not appreciated how lucky we were. We were *de facto* orphans: our father was murdered, our mother was in Russia and we had no idea whether she would ever return to us. Micky was a mother deprived of children and we filled their place for her.

I never heard Micky complain about the suffering she had endured. She was born at a time when those with a position in society to maintain would go to frightening lengths to hush up any scandal or impropriety. I do not know whether my grandfather knew the truth about Micky when he took her on as governess. How much my mother knew or had been told I shall never discover: she died four years before Nancy

Cardozo's book was written.

As so often, unhappiness has a way of repeating itself. Maud Gonne married John MacBride and for a while they lived in Paris where Maud took Micky's daughter Eileen to live with her. Here MacBride, overshadowed by his involvement in the Republican cause and gradually becoming resentful both of Maud's romantic past and of her greater political acumen, turned increasingly to the cafés of Paris for his comfort. According to Maud Gonne's biographer, returning home drunk one night he sexually assaulted Eileen, a terrified seventeen-year-old. This was the last straw for the marriage of Maud and John MacBride. But, anxious to avoid a scandal and to make some reparation to the injured girl in her protection, Maud arranged for Eileen to marry Joseph Mac-Bride, John's forty-three-year-old brother. In a sense Eileen was more fortunate than her mother and even than Maud Gonne, for Joseph was a loyal and good-natured man.

Eileen and Joseph MacBride went to live in Ireland in Westport, County Mayo, where they had a large family and rarely ventured to Dublin, let alone London. I only met Eileen once, when she came to London in 1937 on a short visit. Some years ago I wrote to her because I was curious to find out what she knew about her mother, and also about my grandfather's visit to Ireland. She replied that she knew nothing about her, as Micky had only been a legend to her, and that she had met my grandfather Zakrevsky only once as a young girl in Maud's flat in Paris in 1904 when he was on a visit from St Petersburg. Eileen was in her eighties when she wrote to me and died shortly afterwards.

Neither Micky nor her daughter bore any apparent resentment against those whose sense of decorum had taken over their lives. Only once did Micky's mask of self-containment and restraint crack, and that was when she was delirious and on her death-bed. Roosi alone heard Micky's angry, bitter and defiant outpourings in the last hours of her life; and perhaps the final irony of the story is that Roosi never understood them, for she spoke no English. Micky kept her secret to the end.

CHAPTER IV
My Father and Mother

Brought up by Micky and by Aunt Cossé at Kallijärv, we had little contact with the momentous events that were taking place in the world around us. That world had changed drastically, though we did not, as children, realise by how much. Our parents and their lives were dim shadows to us, and the love we should have given them, we gave to others. My father was dead and already almost a legend to me; my memories of him cease with that moment in the nursery when he stood beside my cot: in a sense, frozen in time, always thirty-six. My mother, of whom I saw so little in the first years of my life, was still in Petrograd, and she remained a distant and enigmatic figure to us children.

I was not to learn the truth about those years for a long time: not, in fact, until I came to London in the 1930s. I realised then that in so many ways my mother's life was a portrait of her age. Russian women of that pre-revolutionary generation, it always seems to me, were more resilient than their menfolk. This was certainly true in our family and especially in the case of my mother. Having been brought up in the lap of luxury and then introduced to the splendour of diplomatic life in the days of the Tsar, she had to make immense changes in order to survive. These explain a great deal in her later life, around which so many stories have grown.

Hers was a family around which myths grew; and although I never knew him, my maternal grandfather Ignatiy Platonovich Zakrevsky represented a similar character, an impulsive and imprudent man who led a larger than life existence. By all accounts he had a strong personality and a good intellect, but his character had been spoilt from childhood by enormous wealth, which induced over-confidence in his own powers. He was often arrogant and extremely intolerant of fools, but he was also independent-minded and known for his liberal outlook and fearlessness in expressing his beliefs.

Grandfather Zakrevsky was a wealthy landowner with a large estate in the district of Poltava in the Ukraine, which was and still is an integral part of the Russian empire. Originally part of the Lithuanian Polish empire, the Ukraine, or Little Russia as it was called in Imperial Russian times, fought for independence against both Poland and Moscow in the eighteenth century. But it was unsuccessful, and was divided up between these two states, and in the end, after the partition of Poland, between Russia and Austria. The landlords in the part which came under Russia, which included Poltava, were fiercely loyal to the Tsar and many of them had official positions in the central government, even though there was a strong feeling of separatism among the people and a pride in their separate cultural heritage.

The Zakrevsky estate was estimated to cover an area of several thousand acres and included large forests and a sugar factory. Many acres of park and gardens surrounded the large white house, built in the classical style with an imposing porch and four substantial columns. Beriozovaya Rudka, as it was called, was approached by an impressive drive lined with silver birch trees ending in a circular lawn, round which the carriages had to drive before leaving their passengers in front of the porch.

In 1876 grandfather Zakrevsky married my grandmother Maria Boreisha and had a son and three daughters. The youngest, born in 1893, eight years after her twin sisters Alla and Assia and twelve years after her brother Platon, known as Bobik, was my mother, Moura. Zakrevsky was proud of his beautiful and bright twin daughters, but Moura was the favourite toy of his middle age and he spoilt her unashamedly. Micky used to tell how, to her dismay, when Moura was about six or seven, her father would call for her to be brought in late in the evening after entertaining official guests. He would then stand her on the table and get her to recite a poem by Pushkin or even a French poem, to the applause of the admiring if sometimes disapproving male gathering. This was the kind of attention and applause she demanded and continued to demand, and was incensed when she did not get – but more often than not she did. Moura's mother, too, transferred all her affection to Moura, almost to the point of neglecting her other children. Moura could do no wrong, and from infancy she became the centre of the household in the vast Ukrainian estate, with servants, governesses and tutors to look after her every need.

My grandfather was bitterly disappointed with his son Bobik. Bobik had none of his vitality and forcefulness. Indeed, he longed only to live a life of ease on the estate. But my grandfather would not have this and forced him against his will into the diplomatic service. Grandfather was not a tolerant man in his relationships with people, and Bobik was no match for his powerful personality. He felt intimidated and inadequate in his presence.

My grandfather had studied law in St Petersburg and also in Berlin and at Heidelberg University. By the age of thirty-four he had written many important articles on the Russian judicial system and legal procedures, and had already been appointed Vice-President of the St Petersburg District Court. He was a Justice of the Peace in St Petersburg until 1873, having joined the Ministry of Justice, and later was appointed President of the Warsaw District Court. In 1881 he became prosecutor at the Court of Justice of the Kazan region and later of the Kharkov region.

He had a masterful personality and was endowed with a sharp, quick brain. But he was too impulsive, partly due to his own indefatigable energy. He had had a broad education, and had travelled widely in Europe, having learned many languages, including French, English, German and Arabic. One of his ambitions was to introduce trial by jury into Russia.

In 1894 my grandfather became chief prosecutor for the Senate with the title of Senator. But his hold on this position was short-lived; for the Dreyfus Affair, which was coming to a climax in France, dividing the country between the Catholic right-wing and the anti-clerical left, proved the undoing of my grandfather's career. Given his character and beliefs, it was inevitable that he should involve himself deeply in the affair. As a liberal, he naturally sided with the left-wing forces that were endeavouring to overturn the verdict and get Dreyfus back from Devil's Island where he had been imprisoned; but even more, he deplored the anti-Semitism which he felt was at the heart of Dreyfus's conviction for espionage. Most important, however, was my grandfather's passionate belief in trial by jury. Engaged as he was in trying to change the Russian legal system in that direction, he was deeply shocked by the procedure of the original trial in France, a court martial held behind closed doors, where damning evidence was given only to the judges and not produced in the trial (evidence that was, in any case, fraudulent), and by the subsequent lies and cover-up. Everything that he believed in was affronted by the Dreyfus Affair, and being the impulsive man he was, he soon made his feelings known.

He addressed an extremely sharp letter to the London *Times* written in French, protesting against Captain Dreyfus's conviction and criticising the way the French authorities had handled the case; and this letter was published in full on September 21st, 1899, in its original French. It was considered most improper for a Russian Senator to make such a declaration and to be interfering openly in French internal politics at a time when relations between France and Russia were particularly sensitive. But not content with having signed this inflammatory letter, Zakrevsky was also involved in a clandestine meeting of supporters of Dreyfus in Paris at the house of Émile Zola, who was the most distinguished literary opponent of the establishment and supporter of Dreyfus in the powerful movement for a re-trial. Invited to attend this meeting, Zakrevsky expressed his views openly and again voiced his criticism of the French military authorities. One of the other guests afterwards reported what Zakrevsky had said to someone in an official position. Complaints were made through diplomatic channels and Zakrevsky had to resign. His career as one of Russia's leading lawyers was shattered. But he continued to take an interest in politics, and foresaw the 1905 Revolution. He wrote mostly about aspects of social and judicial reform, and in several articles published in 1904 he warned the government against its complacency. Early in 1905 he set off on a long journey to Egypt with his twin daughters, my Aunts Assia and Alla. There he died suddenly of a heart attack near Khartoum just before the 1905 Revolution. He was only sixty-four.

There was one story which we often heard told as children, which sums up his colourful personality. Although serfdom in Russia had been abolished in 1861, there was no contact or thought of equality between landowning and peasant classes. My grandfather, however, passionately believed that all human beings deserved equal respect, and in a typically impulsive gesture to demonstrate his conviction he sent his coachman in an open droshky one morning to the home of a peasant, where he was to pick up the labourer's wife and daughter and bring them to the Great House. Here they were given beautiful clothes to wear, after which my grandfather seated himself between the two women and drove them back home. When they reached the peasant's home he helped them from the carriage, bowed and publicly kissed the mother's hand and drove home again. My poor grandmother, an utterly conventional snob, was horrified. He had three possible motives for doing this. The first was indeed a liberal humanitarian reason, but it seems equally probable that this was a deliberate attempt to annoy his wife and shock her out of her narrow-mindedness. However, the most likely reason was that my grandfather was unable to resist pretty girls, and the prospect of a droshky-drive with two beautiful women he could not refuse. Whatever the motive, it remained a talking point in the village for many years afterwards.

Moura was twelve years old at the time of my grandfather's death, and my grandmother decided to leave St Petersburg (though not to sell the apartment there) and to take her to Beriozovaya Rudka, in the Ukraine. My grandmother's move must have been prompted by the fact that life would be less expensive there, for her husband's will had been a terrible shock to her. A Freemason himself, he had left a large part of his personal fortune for the funding of a Freemasonry Lodge in

Scotland. In the Ukraine Moura was taught by tutors and governesses, instead of going to the fashionable Obolensky Institute in St Petersburg which Alla and Assia had attended; but she was deprived, not only of her father's influence, but also of the devotion of one of her most steadfast admirers. She was to remain there for six increasingly frustrated years.

Life with my grandmother had never been easy for any of her children and my grandfather's death made it even more difficult. Bobik fared as badly with her as he had done with his father. When he was born she had doted on him, but as he failed to prove himself the brilliant son she had expected, she, like her husband, withdrew her love from him and in fact neglected him completely. When her twin daughters were born five years later she was equally partial in her love. Alla, from the first, was an incontestable beauty, Assia's good looks developed later. All the disappointment my grandmother had experienced with Bobik was compensated by Alla's beauty, and for eight years it was Alla who received all her love and attention. But in 1893 my mother was born and Alla, just as Bobik before her, was pushed aside by her mother, and the baby became the centre of attention. It must have been an uncomfortable atmosphere for the older children. Bobik was reluctantly beginning his diplomatic career at the Russian Embassy in Tokyo; Aunt Alla wanted nothing more than to be a pianist but was prevented from this by her parents. Assia, probably the most intelligent of the three, had only one intention, to leave home as soon as possible. There were terrible rows between my grandmother and Alla, and my grandmother, to make matters worse, was in the habit of changing the girls' rooms every other week, in the course of which she would throw out any little personal possessions which she considered they did not need.

Assia had no intention of burying herself miles away in the country, and had fallen in love with a charming but physically delicate young man in the diplomatic service, Nikolai Ionoff. She knew that Ionoff was about to be posted to the Russian Embassy in Berlin, where she believed that together they would be able to create a new life for themselves. As it

1 & 2 *Above:* Grandfather and grandmother Zakrevsky
3 *Below left:* Micky at the Beriozovaya Rudka estate, 1908
4 *Below right:* The summer house on the estate

5 *Left:* Djon von Benckendorff in the uniform of the Lycée
6 *Below:* The Great House at Yendel

7 *Above:* Djon and Moura leave Yendel for St Petersburg in 1912
8 *Left:* Aunt Assia at the Potsdam Court ball in 1912

9 Moura and Djon at the races in Berlin, 1913

happened, Bobik had also been posted from Tokyo to the Russian Embassy in Berlin as an assistant First Secretary. Assia became secretly engaged to Ionoff and, realising that her mother was unlikely to give her consent to a quick wedding, she eloped with him. For Alla, Assia's marriage in 1907 was a terrible blow. Not only did it deprive her of an ally, it also strengthened my grandmother's resolve to keep her other two daughters with her in Beriozovaya Rudka. But in the same year Alla also married and went to live in Nice.

By the time Moura was seventeen the family circle had shrunk considerably and she was thoroughly bored and restless. She wrote to Assia in Berlin complaining about this, and her sister replied inviting her to stay. 'Bring your smartest clothes as there will be plenty of parties, Court balls and other functions to go to,' Assia wrote. The Berlin Embassy was considered to be the most prestigious of all Russian embassies and it certainly had the most active social life. It must therefore have seemed particularly attractive to Moura in the depths of the country, abandoned by the rest of her family and seeking new conquests ... In her letter Assia had casually mentioned that a friend of Bobik's from the St Petersburg Lycée days had recently joined the staff of the embassy – Ioann (Djon) Alexandrovich von Benckendorff – and would make a perfect escort for her younger sister. My grandmother finally agreed to let Moura go, entrusting her to the care of her sister and brother-in-law, and she left to spend a month in Berlin.

Djon was twenty-eight and my mother was eighteen. He was immediately drawn to this young, lively and attractive girl, and before long was very much in love with her. It seemed the perfect match and surprised nobody that they should marry. As the eldest son, Djon had recently inherited his father's large estate in the province of Estonia and he looked forward to taking his young bride there. Socially, too, the marriage was a suitable one, approved by both friends and relatives. Even Micky, to whom the Zakrevskys meant everything and who had no love for Djon's Baltic relatives, was very fond of Djon, as was my maternal grandmother.

Djon was very much a product of his conventional background. The Benckendorff family traced their origin back to the Order of the Teutonic Knights, who in the fourteenth century drove out the Danes and brought Christianity to the territories known later as the Baltic States. Throughout seven centuries this area had been under foreign domination: first it was ruled by the Danes, then by the Teutonic Knights, then by the Swedes, and these were followed by 200 years of Russian rule. It was Peter the Great who incorporated the Baltic provinces into the Russian empire on the understanding that the Baltic landowners retained their privileges and powers. The Baltic nobility to which my father belonged maintained their position as the landowning class in the area until the end of the First World War, and were deeply attached to the estates they had held since 1346. The first member of the Benckendorff family to achieve political prominence was Johann Benckendorff, who became Burgomaster of Riga in 1657 and was ennobled in 1674 by King Charles XI of Sweden. The tradition of service to Russia was later exemplified by the career of another member of the Benckendorff family, General Alexander von Benckendorff (1781-1844), who became Chief of Police under Tsar Nicholas I, and for this perhaps dubious distinction received the additional title of Count in 1832. He had been responsible for the supervision of the liberal sympathisers – including the poet Alexander Pushkin – who were exiled after the abortive Decembrist uprising in 1821. At about the same time his first cousin, my great-great-grandfather Paul Friedrich von Benckendorff, was elected Knight Commander of the province of Estonia, and was appointed Civil Governor to administer Estonia on behalf of the Russian Government. The Benckendorffs, like all other Baltic families, were loyal supporters of the Tsar until the abdication of Nicholas II and the revolution of 1917.

My father had been groomed for service in the Imperial Russian Administration and educated at the Imperial Lycée in St Petersburg. The Lycée had been set up by Catherine the Great and reserved for sons of noblemen and high-ranking officials. These were often chosen from the Baltic aristocracy. Boys entered at the age of twelve and were educated up to university standard. It was, in effect, a training school for the higher levels of the administration. My father did extremely well and passed out near the top of his year. In 1908 he joined the Russian diplomatic service in the Ministry of Foreign Affairs and in the same year was appointed Chamberlain to the Court of the Tsar in St Petersburg and was also made a Privy Councillor. In 1909 he was sent to the Russian Embassy in Berlin. There, by all accounts, he earned the respect of everyone who came into contact with him as a diplomat of charm and promise. The only contemporary letter relating to my father's career is from my grandfather, written to a cousin of his on August 17th, 1910 when my father was twenty-seven years old. He writes:

> My son in Berlin has just been with me to buy some carriage horses for his Ambassador. This summer he was nominated for the post of Second Secretary in Constantinople but at the earnest request of the Russian Ambassador in Berlin he was promoted to the same rank at the Embassy there. The intervention of the Ambassador shows that my son is indispensable to him and is a remarkable testimony to his capability.

He was also a brave and fearless man: the story remained in my family that he had once, at the age of seventeen, ridden alone on horseback from Reval to St Petersburg, a distance of 200 miles.

Moura married without being in love or knowing the demands that marriage makes: she had always been happy to be adored, and few people had asked her to give anything in return. She was attracted by the glamour of a diplomatic marriage, which gave her unrivalled social opportunities. At one Court ball at the Potsdam Palace she and Assia were presented to the Tsar. Such a strong impression did they make in their beautiful Court dresses, with gold-studded trains and traditional Russian head-dress studded with pearls, that Assia heard the Crown Prince exclaim 'Quelle noblesse!'

After my mother's marriage in 1911 she spent the next three

years principally in Berlin where Djon continued to work at the embassy. Life at the embassy was a mixture of high-level diplomacy and glamorous social functions. There are very few pictures remaining of my parents together, but one taken of them at the races in Potsdam shows them off very well: my father stiff and formal, but kindly; my mother very much the young bride and social success. My parents acquired a beautiful apartment in St Petersburg where they entertained lavishly when on leave. The carefree and luxurious life of the Russian Embassy in Berlin came to an abrupt, if foreseeable, end in August 1914 when war broke out. The Russian Ambassador, Count von Osten-Sacken, and his staff were recalled to St Petersburg and the Benckendorff family returned to Russia. Moura was now pregnant for the second time (my brother was born in Yendel in 1913). Quite soon Djon decided to enlist in the army and was appointed Staff Officer at the headquarters of the Northern Russian Army.

There were no official parties or embassy balls for the duration of the war, but right up to the October 1917 Revolution it was possible to maintain the outward appearances of social life, and restaurants and gypsy taverns were increasingly patronised in the absence of formal social functions. Although my father was away in the army, my mother was still enjoying what remained of a social life in Petrograd. It was usual to move households once or twice a year to their country estates; and my mother continued to spend her summers on the estate at Yendel as they had done in the years before the war. It was also possible to get away to Yendel for long weekends from Petrograd. The original house had been destroyed by fire and the new house was built at the centre of the estate in red brick in the style of a fortified castle with a large turret. Although it may seem rather strange to us to have built such a house in the twentieth century, it was most suitable for entertaining, with its huge reception rooms, imposing staircase and more than forty rooms. It was here that my parents would come every summer; and it was here, away from the formality of the embassy, the Court and the army, that they enjoyed the company of their own friends. When they were in residence the house was always filled with visitors. Baron and Baroness Stackelberg often came from Finland, my father's brother Paul and his wife from Reval, Baroness Schilling, Bobby Yonin and Miriam Artimovich from Petrograd, and of course many others whose names I do not know. Perhaps because of my mother's command of English (due to Micky's teaching), among the guests who often came at weekends were members of the British Embassy staff in Petrograd to whom Moura had become closely attached during my father's absence on military service. In her memoirs Meriel Buchanan, the daughter of the British Ambassador in Petrograd, Sir George Buchanan, recalls with delight her visits to Yendel in the years before the revolution. She speaks of lively and carefree long weekends, the snow-covered landscape, the jingle of bells from a sleigh bringing supplies to the Great House from the farm; the sudden impulsive plans to visit Reval or organise a fancy dress ball; the drives in troikas through the woods. The picture that she gives is of young high-spirited people, apparently untroubled by approaching cataclysmic changes. On what was probably Meriel Buchanan's last visit in the summer of 1917 the house-party was joined by several officers from the British naval expedition in the Baltic: these included Captain Francis Cromie, the young Naval Attaché who was later killed on the steps of the British Embassy resisting the entry of the Cheka (Secret Police) officials, and Dennis Garstin, a young cavalry officer, who was to be an important friend of my mother's. They were not permanent members of the embassy staff, but had been sent by the Admiralty to see that the Russian Baltic fleet did not fall into the hands of the Germans.

What is remarkable is that although the Russian Revolution had already begun, with the abdication of the Tsar and the establishment of the Provisional Government under Kerensky in March 1917, life at Yendel that summer seems to have gone on quite as before. Although perhaps not distinguished as a poem, Dennis Garstin's account in verse of life at Yendel that summer, and his fond memories of it, show how far it was from the political realities of the day:

At Yendel girls begin the day
In optimistic negligée
Followed hot-footed, after ten,
By the pyjama radiant men.
… but I'll be sad
In Petrograd, in Petrograd,
Thinking of many a happy ride
Astride the liniaker …
Or how we danced the good night through
Or in hallucination flew
On aeroplanes, and how the Devil
Inspired the maids to go to Reval
Rebreaking tender sailors' hearts …
Oh God, and I must take a train
And go to Petrograd again,
And while I deal out propaganda
My nicer thoughts will all meander
Back, back to Yendel, oh to be
In Yendel for eternity.

The crash came only a few months after this was written.

The establishment of the Provisional Government in March 1917 had in fact had little immediate effect on everyday life in Petrograd. Although there were rumours of uprisings and discontent in the country and no lack of danger signals of what lay in store, life did not change very much. For many of the well-to-do it was hard to believe that there would be a permanent change in society.

By the time my mother returned from Yendel that summer, it was, however, alarmingly clear that this state of affairs could not last. Soviets were being established within the armed forces and all over Petrograd, and although they were a minority, the power of the Bolsheviks was growing rapidly. In October of that year Kerensky's short-lived Liberal Socialist government was overthrown by the Bolsheviks: chaos and civil war spread throughout Russia. Petrograd society at last woke up to the seriousness of events, and realised that its way of life had gone for ever. Many families abandoned their homes and fled the country; many others were arrested by the Bolsheviks and suffered exile or death.

My father watched the development of events towards the end of 1917 with growing alarm. There were worrying rumours from all parts of the country. By the end of the year it was clear that the revolution was spreading into Estonia, and increasing demands for independence threatened the stability of the estates there. My father realised that he had to return to Yendel to look after his estate. Meriel Buchanan records meeting him in Petrograd at this time, in her autobiography, *Ambassador's Daughter*:

> On Christmas night we invited the members of the staff, as well as all the Naval and Military Missions and a few intimate Russian friends, to what was to be the last party ever given in the British Embassy in Petrograd. Luckily it was an evening when the electricity was not cut off, so the crystal chandeliers blazed with light as they had done in the past and although the ballroom was stacked with tins of bully beef and other provisions, although every officer there had a loaded pistol in his pocket, and there were rifles and cartridge cases hidden in the Chancery, we tried to forget the desolate streets and the threat of constant danger. We played the piano and sang songs, we drank champagne and laughed, to hide the sadness in all our hearts. Moura was there with her husband who, now that the Russian Army was no longer fighting, had come back, and was only a few months later to be killed by the peasants at Yendel. Dennis Garstin was there, and Captain Cromie who, having blown up the submarines and sent the crews home, had consented very unwillingly to remain on at the Embassy as Naval Attaché. At the end of the evening, someone – I think it was Miriam's fiancé, Bobby Yonin – began to play the Russian National Anthem, and a sudden, almost breathless silence fell on the crowded room. I was trying not to remember the many times I had heard that Anthem played in the past, but happening to glance at Moura's husband and seeing the

look of suffering on his face, I could no longer hold back my
tears.

I was indeed finding it very difficult not to cry all during
those last two weeks. Day after day I went to say goodbye to
one more building, to one more place which had become
dear and familiar.

My father had always impressed everyone by his strict sense
of honour and decency, and the collapse of all that he held dear
must have been terrible for him. The Tsar, to whom he had
given his allegiance and to whom he had been a personal aide-
de-camp, was a prisoner of the Bolsheviks; the values for
which he had fought were in ruins.

He left for Estonia early in the New Year. We children were
to follow later with my mother and Micky. We set off for
Yendel in the late spring, but Moura remained in Petrograd
saying that she intended to follow as soon as she had made
arrangements for her mother's safety. Her mother, who was
living in Petrograd in her apartment in Spalernaya Street with
her personal maid, Natalia, and a cook, was very ill. Meanwhile Moura remained in contact with Dennis Garstin and
other members of the British Embassy staff. It was through
Garstin that, within days of the departure of her children, she
met the man who was to have the most profound effect on her
life.

In March 1918, at a party given in Petrograd for Dennis
Garstin's birthday, she was introduced to Robert Bruce
Lockhart.

CHAPTER V
Robert Bruce Lockhart

Robert Bruce Lockhart knew Russia well. After an adventurous and somewhat disastrous start as a planter in Malaya, he had passed the general consular service exam and been posted in 1912 as Vice-Consul in Moscow. Before leaving for Russia he had become engaged to an Australian girl whom he returned to marry a year later. The Consul-General at the time, Clive Bayley, had no knowledge of the Russian language and consequently relied on Lockhart to a great extent for his political intelligence and contacts. As a result, the Lockharts made many friends among the leading families of Moscow and politicians of different convictions. When the Consul-General had to return to England for reasons of health in 1915, the Ambassador, Sir George Buchanan, persuaded the Foreign Office not to replace him, but to let Lockhart, who was then only twenty-seven, serve as 'acting Consul-General for the duration of the war' in what was rapidly becoming one of the most important British posts abroad.

With the fall of Warsaw in the summer campaign of 1915 Lockhart had already become convinced of the impending tragedy for Russia. He saw that the initial enthusiasm for war had been destroyed by the defeat at Tannenberg and the failure of the advance into Austria; in its place he found political unease, growing resentment against the alleged pro-German sentiments of the government due to the interference of the Tsarina, and against the influence on her of Rasputin, and disorder among new conscripts to the army. During 1916 all hopes of a military victory disappeared, and further defeats brought even closer the expected political cataclysm.

Lockhart described the situation in Petrograd which he visited at the end of 1916:

I found the atmosphere more depressing than ever. Champagne flowed like water. The Astoria and the Europa – the two best hotels in the capital – were thronged with officers who had been at the front. There was no disgrace in being the 'shirker' or in finding a sinecure in the rear. I had the impression of senseless ennui and fin de siècle. And in the streets were the long queues of ill-clad men and garrulous women, waiting for the bread which never came.

On March 12th, 1917 the storm broke and according to Lockhart, 'In a night a bread riot similar to hundreds which had taken place during the previous twelve months had become a revolution. In Moscow there was no bloodshed. There was no one left to defend the old régime.' Lockhart went on to say:

My own contact with the first revolution lasted for eight months. It was a period of depression and disintegration, of a new activity from which all hope and faith had gone. I had been an admirer of the old régime but I had little difficulty in realising what the effect of the new must be on the war.

For Lockhart it was clear that only a party which offered peace rather than war could succeed. Prince Lvov, the first Prime Minister of the Provisional Government, was followed by Alexander Kerensky who was unable to stem the ever more strident demands, principally from the army which was strongly influenced by the Bolsheviks, for peace. Matters were clearly growing to a head: the German army was steadily advancing, and in August the Tsar, who had abdicated in March and been sent to Tsarskoye Selo, was moved with his family to Tobolsk, from where they were subsequently taken by the Bolsheviks to Ekaterinburg, where he and his family were all murdered. The Russian army was on the brink of defeat.

Meanwhile Lockhart's personal affairs had interfered with his career. 'Just as the old Russia was advancing inevitably to her final tragedy so, too, there was a minor tragedy in my own life.' In September 1917 he was recalled to London. In his own words the recall was 'owing to an attachment I had formed with a Russian Jewess'. To avoid a scandal he had been granted sick-leave from Moscow by the British Ambassador, Sir George Buchanan, and had returned to London with his wife, six weeks before the Bolshevik October Revolution.

After his return to London Lockhart had been able to convince the members of the government that the Bolshevik Revolution was not likely to be a short-lived affair and that it was unwise to consider that Lenin and Trotsky were merely German agents with little or no popular support. He insisted that it was necessary to establish and maintain some regular contact with the men who were now directing Russia's destiny. Lloyd George himself decided that Bruce Lockhart was the right man to head a mission to Soviet Russia.

Lockhart selected as members of his mission Captain William Hicks, who had recently returned from Russia where he had been working as a poison gas expert, Edward Birse, a Moscow businessman who had a good knowledge of Russian, and Edward Phelan of the Ministry of Labour, who later became Director-General of the International Labour Office. In 1932, Bruce Lockhart described the purpose of his mission in his hugely successful book *Memoirs of a British Agent*. The book is a first-hand account by one who was very much involved at the time, and gives a full picture of Bruce Lockhart's life from his first arrival in Russia until his expulsion in 1918. Lloyd George sent him back to Soviet Russia in early 1918 with the express intention of establishing direct contact with the Bolsheviks, of doing as much damage as possible to the German cause, and stiffening Russian resistance and their resolve to continue the war. To this end he attempted to put a spoke in the negotiations for a separate peace between Russia and Germany which had begun in Brest-Litovsk. The Bolsheviks were themselves divided on the question of a separate peace with Germany. Lenin was for peace at any price, as he considered that only through a peace could he consolidate his position. Trotsky, on the other hand, would have been prepared to continue the war if he could have been certain of Allied intervention, but at that time Lockhart was unable to obtain any commitment from the British Government.

In view of the continuing advance into Russia of the German armies it was decided by the Allies that their embassies should be evacuated. Lockhart was able to obtain visas for all members of the British Embassy. The Allied embassies left Petrograd on February 28th, but Lockhart retained as members of his mission two embassy officials, Captain Cromie who was Naval Attaché, determined not to let the Baltic fleet into the hands of the Germans, and Dennis Garstin who had a good knowledge of Russia.

On March 3rd, 1918, the preliminary peace treaty was signed at Brest-Litovsk and the next day a meeting in Moscow of the Congress of all the Soviets was convened for March 12th, to give its formal approval to the treaty. At the same time a new Supreme War Council with Trotsky as President was created. The decision to convene the meeting of the Congress of all the Soviets in Moscow meant that the government would evacuate Petrograd and move to Moscow. Lockhart stayed behind in Petrograd for another week while he waited for Trotsky, who had promised to supervise personally the transport and to find accommodation for the British mission in Moscow.

In *Memoirs of a British Agent* Lockhart wrote:

> It was at this time that I first met Moura who was an old friend of Hicks and Garstin and a frequent visitor to our flat. She was then twenty-five. A Russian of the Russians, she had a lofty disregard for all the pettiness of life and a courage which was proof against all cowardice ... During those first days of our meeting in St Petersburg I was too busy, too preoccupied with my own importance to give her more than a passing thought ... the romance was to come afterwards.

At the end of that week Lockhart left for Moscow and they wrote to each other regularly. A month later Moura came to stay in the flat in Moscow occupied by the British mission.

'From then on,' wrote Lockhart, 'she was never to leave us until we were parted by the armed force of the Bolsheviks.'

To her he appeared charming, witty, knowledgeable and full of life. And above all he loved and understood Russia. He spoke fluent Russian and had strong views about the future of Russia, based on a deep knowledge of the political situation. She was twenty-five and he was thirty-two. It was a time for heightened emotions: great things were happening in Russia, and the climate in which Lockhart and Moura found themselves was a fertile one for adventure. They must have had the feeling that war and revolution inevitably create – that you should get out of life what you can today because there may be no tomorrow.

In the summer of 1918 Lockhart was finding himself to be in increasing disagreement with the British Government over the question of Allied intervention in Russia. At first he was violently opposed to it and warned the British Government that the Bolsheviks were there to stay and that intervention without their consent would only result in civil war. He sensed that he was earning the reputation in London of being pro-Bolshevik. In his book he recounted his thoughts of resignation which he eventually put aside. 'Subconsciously,' he wrote, 'although I did not put the question to myself I was unwilling to leave because of Moura.'

During this period the position of the Allied missions in Moscow was becoming more and more difficult. In July an attempted *coup d'état* by the Left Social Revolutionaries involving the murder of the German Ambassador, Count Mirbach, failed. They had differed from the Bolsheviks on the signing of the Treaty of Brest-Litovsk and on their whole attitude towards the Germans. After the failure of the plot, the Bolsheviks strengthened their grip on the country and imprisoned the leaders of the Left Social Revolutionaries. On July 17th Lockhart was one of the first foreign diplomats to hear of the murder of the Tsar and his family at Ekaterinburg. A few days later news came of the departure of the Allied embassies from Vologda to Archangel.

Although not informed of the move beforehand, the British

mission in Moscow interpreted this as being a prelude to
military intervention. Lockhart wrote in his book:

> It was, however, clear that our own position in Moscow was
> no longer tenable and I returned to my rooms to take the
> preliminary steps for our departure. The next few days were
> the most miserable of my whole stay in Russia. Moura had
> left Moscow some ten days before to visit her home in
> Estonia. Owing to the fighting on the Czech and Yaroslavl
> fronts [on the Volga north of Moscow] travelling on the
> railways was now strictly controlled. I could not communi-
> cate with her. It seemed any odds on my having to leave
> Russia without seeing her again ... There was nothing we
> could do and I abandoned myself to the gloomiest depres-
> sion. Then, on the afternoon of July 28th my telephone
> rang. Moura herself was talking. She had arrived in
> Petrograd after six days of terrible adventure crossing the
> no-man's-land between Estonia and Russia. The reaction
> was wonderful. Nothing now mattered ...

But Lockhart gives no explanation for Moura's short-lived
stay in Estonia. Why had she gone at a time when the situation
in Moscow was becoming really difficult? Why had she been
prepared to face the journey to Estonia when that country was
still under German occupation after the signing of the Treaty
of Brest-Litovsk, and why after facing these hazards would she
return to Petrograd and then to Moscow after such a short
time?

Just before leaving for Estonia Moura wrote to Lockhart
from Petrograd:

> I am capable of braving anything for your sake, I love you
> more than all the world ... I am going as you know for the
> sake of 'little Peter', to play a repulsive part which will lead
> to repulsive consequences and I shall have to stick to them
> for nine months, war or no war ... You need not have any
> fear that I will regret anything and I have complete con-
> fidence in you ... Nine months of hypocrisy and then I will

be free to make a clean breast of it ... Now I am also hoping against hope that I will see you again before you have to go. I will be back here [Petrograd] by next Saturday and will come to Moscow immediately.

After crossing the demarcation line into Estonia she wrote from Narva (undated but probably a day or two later):

... I don't know how I have been able to bear this day – it is only the thought of little Peter which has helped me through. First the despair of leaving you ... Fancy, since 5.30 a.m. today we have been out on the road driving *au pas*, stopping, driving again ... Goodbye my only love ...

A day or two later still:

Saturday. I am writing you this from Yendel. It is still worse than I thought ... I've got to stand a German officer at lunch and dinner – and it is torture. It's unfair, it's unfair – and at times I want to scream and say I am not going to bear it any more. It is only the thought of him, of our little boy that stops me – but I don't know, Babykins, if I'll be able to stick to it after all ... I'm only thinking of how to get back ... '

These letters show clearly that Moura had become pregnant. She wanted at all costs to prove that she had had contact with her husband during the beginning of her pregnancy in order to avoid the stigma of illegitimacy for the child. To spend a week with her husband in Estonia was the only solution. This 'deception', she argued, would involve playing a part for nine months which would be unpleasant but had to be endured. After that period she would be prepared to leave her children to her husband, obtain a divorce, and follow Lockhart to the end of the world ...

But by September she had lost the child. Exactly when that happened is not clear. Judging from the contents of a note written to Lockhart in that month it was probably some time during his imprisonment in Moscow. The note was given to him in prison. In a clear reference to the loss of the baby she begs him not to be too worried by what has happened, as it would only upset her more. From then they were able to plan their meeting in Stockholm after his departure from Russia, and it is to this that her later letters constantly refer.

But events had moved faster than they had foreseen. The work of the British mission in Moscow had come to a sudden end when in August 1918 a young Jewish Social Revolutionary girl, Dora Kaplan, had fired two shots point-blank at Lenin as he was leaving a factory. One bullet pierced a lung, the other entered the neck near to the main artery. They had not killed the Russian leader but his chances of survival seemed to be in serious doubt.

The reaction of the Bolshevik Government was immediate. Lockhart and Captain Hicks were arrested in the flat and detained for the night by Cheka agents in the Liubyanka prison, but were released on the orders of Chicherin, then Foreign Minister. When Lockhart returned to his flat he learned that Moura, as well as his servants, had also been taken off by the Cheka but had not yet been released. He decided to go in person to see Peters, the Cheka official who had been directly responsible for him during his one night's detention in the Liubyanka prison. He went straight to the prison where he was promptly rearrested by Peters. Moura was released a few days later when Peters had satisfied himself that she was not implicated in the 'Lockhart Plot', and she was allowed to visit Lockhart in prison.

On September 2nd an official statement was published in *Izvestia* alleging a 'conspiracy of Allied Imperialists against Soviet Russia headed by Bruce Lockhart and the French Consul-General Lavergne'. The purpose of the conspiracy, it was alleged, was to organise the capture of the Council of People's Commissars and to proclaim a military dictatorship. The plot had been revealed by the Lettish garrison which the Allies had attempted to bribe. On the same day as Lockhart was arrested in Moscow, Captain Cromie was killed on the steps of the British Embassy in Petrograd resisting an incursion by Cheka agents. All the other British officials in Petrograd had also been arrested.

Lockhart's imprisonment lasted one month. His fate appeared in doubt at first. But Lenin's recovery brought about a change in the official attitude of the Bolsheviks. Lockhart's release was eventually secured by the intervention of the British Government and the promise of his exchange for Maxim Litvinoff, the official representative of the Bolshevik régime in London. When the negotiations for the exchange were completed, Lockhart was given two days to pack before leaving Russia for good. It was finally agreed that Lockhart and the other members of the mission would be allowed to leave Russian soil when Litvinoff had reached Bergen in Norway.

The blow of Lockhart's departure in October was partly softened for Moura by the friendship of Alan Wardwell in the four weeks that remained before he too left Russia for good. A distinguished New York lawyer, he was a member of the American Red Cross Commission to Russia responsible for the shipments of food to Murmansk, which were then brought to Petrograd and Moscow. He had worked closely with Lockhart and had helped to secure the release of a number of British officials after the attempt on Lenin's life, dealing with tact and skill with the Soviet authorities. His intervention with the Bolsheviks on behalf of the British subjects received the official recognition of the British Government, in the form of a silver plate which Lord Curzon, then Foreign Secretary, requested the American Ambassador in London to send to him. Wardwell's friendship was also of great importance to Moura. He accompanied her from the station when Lockhart left, and acted as a courier for their letters over the next four weeks. This kindness forged a link between our two families that has lasted even to the present day; in 1940 he sponsored Kira and her two children to come to America to escape the war, and later his grandson Eddie lived with us in London when he was a postgraduate student at Oxford.

Lockhart wrote in his *Memoirs* that 'Moura had accepted their parting with Russian fatalism. She knew that there was no other way.' What Lockhart did not say, and what is clear from her letters, is that he and Moura had made a firm plan to meet in Sweden before the end of the year. She had agreed to wait for him in Petrograd till she got word to join him in Stockholm. There they would be together till she was able to arrange a divorce from her husband and he from his wife; then they would be together for good. Now that she had lost their child they could be united very soon, she firmly believed. But although a few letters arrived from Lockhart during the next three or four months, they made no mention of their promised reunion in Stockholm. Letters took a long time to arrive. Moura was overjoyed on receiving three in February 1919 which had been written on December 18th and January 16th. Later she wrote, 'I got three letters from you today – at last! ... What sad troubled little letters. How I wish I were with you to try and make things easier ... ' These appear to have been the last letters she received. She continued to write to him regularly, always wondering whether her letters were reaching him. She did not want to return to her husband even if there was no risk in crossing the frontier to Estonia, which was not yet a fully independent state, the borders being still undefined. So she remained in Petrograd, hoping and waiting for news from Lockhart.

The other members of the mission and journalists had already left Russia taking with them their Russian wives. Benji Bruce had returned to Russia to fetch his wife, the famous ballerina Tamara Karsavina, and Captain Hicks had managed to marry Liuba Malinina the night before they left on the same train as Lockhart for Finland. And there was Arthur Ransome, then *Manchester Guardian* correspondent, who also took a Russian wife home with him.

On November 11th, 1918 the Armistice between the western Allies and Germany was signed. The trial of the conspirators in the so-called Lockhart Plot began on November 28th. The tribunal sentenced Lockhart and Reilly of the British mission and Grenard and Lavergne of the French mission to death 'in absentia'. Civil war was now raging in the south, and in the north-west General Yudenich was threatening Petrograd.

Letters written by Moura in February 1919 (four months after Lockhart's departure) show how much she was still counting on their agreed reunion in Stockholm.

February 10th:
… What if you should be prevented from coming to Stockholm for a short time? That one idea haunts me now day and night. Oh, if only it could come true, my plan …

February 14th:
We are going to meet in Stockholm, pray God in a month or perhaps sooner and then everything will be clear. I am having a hard time, but it will all be swept away the minute I am with you again – and then nothing will matter. To be together, that is the main point. What we shall do afterwards is of inferior importance …

An earlier letter had again referred to 'little Peter' and Moura wrote:

… I want to say to you how it weighs on me to feel that I have come and interfered with all your life. And what have I given you? If little Peter had remained – it would have been something …

She lived for the reunion with Lockhart. She had promised to wait in Russia and it was only the prospect of meeting him again and being permanently united with him in Stockholm that kept her going. She continued to write to him. Two years later in 1921 she received a cold and impersonal letter, saying that he had had a son by his wife and making very little reference to his relationship with herself. This letter arrived in Leningrad a day or two before Moura left Russia permanently for Estonia. From Estonia she replied to Lockhart:

Reval June 24th 1921 … I do not know, my Baby, whether I ever will send you this letter … I got the first news from you after two years, the day before I left Russia. What luck, wasn't it – if I hadn't – why, then, naive to the end – I'd have, perhaps, bombarded you with wires – awkward, wouldn't it have been? There is no use asking you why and how and when, is it? – only that there is something in me that aches so intensely that I must shout it out to you. Your son? A fine boy? Do you know – as I write those words – it seems to me that I will not be able to live with that thought. I thought I'd forgotten how to cry. But there was 'little Peter', you know. I have been out of Russia for a month today fighting with the longing to write to you – now I've done it. That's all. Goodbye. Be happy if you can, but I don't think you can quite …

But even though she wrote him this final-sounding letter, she would not give up hope that their relationship could somehow continue.

In a letter written at the time to her friend Liuba Hicks, Moura said that Lockhart had taught her to look upon the revolution calmly and dispassionately in those early years. He saw it as something inevitable and of world importance, something which had come to stay. Until then her life, like that of most young women of her background and generation, had been sheltered and restricted. Social and economic problems had not concerned her. They were something to be read about in books, but they were not real. Her intellect and her emotions had been dormant. Her marriage to my father had been the natural sequel to a conventional upbringing. Superficially, they had much in common and, had their life continued as it had begun, they might have been contented and happy together. Her relationship with Bruce Lockhart was an eye-opener to a different world. Being in love, she was intoxicated by everything he explained and introduced her to. Suddenly her outlook was being broadened.

Of all the various emotional attachments in the later years of her life, I believe that Robert Bruce Lockhart was probably the only man she really loved. He was the one for whom she was willing to make every sacrifice. Her letters to him at the time show that she was prepared to give up everything for him – her husband, her children, as well as her reputation and even her allegiances – to follow him wherever he said.

In *Memoirs of a British Agent* Lockhart described his relationship with Moura in terms of a great romantic love. No doubt he had been enchanted and very much in love at the time. But in spite of the moving story he tells in his book, I believe – from what I have been told by my mother and others who were there at the time – that for him it was not a consuming passion but a romantic adventure, and perhaps the climax of the most exciting months of his life. The truth is that Lockhart was something of an adventurer and professional charmer, and Russia in 1918 was a place highly conducive to adventure.

When he returned to London and his wife he no longer looked upon his romance with Moura as a lasting relationship to be resumed when they met again. I believe that what he wrote about his love for Moura in his book, which was published fifteen years later, was a romanticised version of what was for him a full-blooded but short-lived affair. For the public it was a sensational love-story against a fascinating political background.

The book was immediately a great success. In a curious way it served as Moura's passport to fame in England. Everywhere she went in English society she was introduced and talked of as the heroine of that book. Later a film based on it, starring Leslie Howard, added to the romance of the legend and finally blurred the distinction between fact and fiction in that period of her life.

When I was given the book to read by my mother at the age of nineteen (soon after my first arrival in London from Estonia via Finland, where I myself had fallen in love, and feeling miserable, interested only in what the post would bring), I had no inkling of there having been anybody in her life except my father while he was alive. I remember thinking what an emotional and exciting affair it must have been for my mother, but how selfish and dreadful it was of Lockhart to have written about it in this way when there were so many people who would be deeply hurt, especially back home. I said this to my mother and I remember her sad and apparently casual reply: 'I know, but without that story the book would not have been such a success and he badly needed the money.'

In spite of that I could see that she was not displeased with the way he had presented their romance in his book. She then told me that he had let her down cruelly, and that the year which followed his departure from Russia had been the only time in her life when she had felt total despair as she waited for letters which never came. I think that she had forgiven him completely by now; and she had no illusions about him by the time the book was published.

They met again in 1923 in Vienna at the Hicks's, after which Lockhart wrote to her that 'the old feeling has gone, never to be revived'. Moura argued with him and tried to bring back their former intimacy; but Lockhart was already otherwise involved. However, they remained good friends to the end of his life, though I think this was due to her insistence rather than to his efforts.

This first experience of being forsaken imbued Moura with a spirit of acceptance of setbacks which stood her in good stead in later life. It was the first time that she had not had her own way. She played down the seriousness of the affair in later years, but her rejection had been hard to accept and had hurt her deeply. There is no doubt that at the time she was shattered by his behaviour, and her disappointment affected her deeply for many years to come. Yet this passionate and eventful affair had in fact lasted no more than eight months, from March to October 1918.

CHAPTER VI
Petrograd

When Robert Bruce Lockhart left Moscow in October 1918 there was nothing for Moura to do but to go back to Petrograd. Her mother was still living in her large apartment; by now a sick woman, she was looked after by her cook and a maid, but her health was failing fast, and Moura returned to be with her. Life in Petrograd was becoming increasingly difficult. Moura's most urgent problem was to realise sufficient money to live on while waiting for news from Lockhart.

The first action that Moura had to take was to deal with her own apartment in the city. House property had been nationalised, but it was still possible to remove things clandestinely before the authorities got around to taking actual possession. Luckily her mother's apartment was not taken over because of her state of health. She was able to stay there until she died. But it was still essential for Moura to raise money, because she was dependent upon the black market at that time. Food was strictly rationed by the Petrograd authorities and in order to acquire the vital ration-card it was necessary to have employment. From a letter to Lockhart at the end of 1918 it is clear that Moura found temporary work in an office, but the job did not last long, and she was forced to sell or barter most of her own and her husband's possessions in order to provide for her essential needs. She spent much time going to different government offices trying to get money to Petrograd from the family estate in the Ukraine, but this proved impossible. The country was in a state of civil war and any contact with the Ukraine was very difficult; so she was forced to go to the money-lenders. Her clothes and personal possessions associated with her former life were gradually sold off in order to buy food; furniture, pictures, even her Court ball gown were bartered or sold cheap.

With Bruce Lockhart, she had been at the very heart of events, stimulated by the excitement of his being in close touch with people who were making history. The life she now faced in Petrograd was very different, for it was simply a battle for personal survival. Her mind was occupied with making plans for the future: all this time she was wondering how best she could obtain a divorce. She refers to this in several letters to Lockhart:

> What a lot has changed since you have sent off these letters ... let me tell you again how things stand with me. I am stuck here on account of Mother, partly, and secondly on account of the impossibility of getting in touch with the Baltic provinces. You see, I've got a few things to settle before clearing out altogether: my divorce of course – then Mother's comparative safety and comfort and money matters in connection with the children. If you could possibly get away for a week to Stockholm, say towards the end of February, I could meet you there ... So Baby – now as four months ago I tell you I am yours – I love you more than life itself ...

But all the time she was haunted by the idea that Lockhart might not be able to meet her in Stockholm as planned. Life must also have been very lonely: many of her former friends had either fled Russia or had been shot by the Bolsheviks; of those that remained most had ostracised her because of her affair with Bruce Lockhart, and rumours that had already begun to attach themselves to her. Garstin and Cromie were dead (Garstin was killed in Archangel where he had been sent by the War Office). She was left very much alone with a sick mother in a city that was becoming increasingly dangerous: her letters of this period contain references to shots and fighting in the city. Without work, enduring constant worries over money and the uncertainty of her future with Lockhart, Moura had to find some outlet to take her mind off things; and it appears that she attended some external courses in law and history, although, as the situation in the city deteriorated, university courses soon came to an end.

Although it is hard to piece together exactly what her life must have been like during the winter of 1918-19, her letters that survive from that period describe the difficulties she faced. She was all the time bolstering herself with the hope that she would soon be reunited with Lockhart and that all this horror would end. But as winter turned to spring the position became even more hopeless. In the middle of May 1919 Moura received news that her husband had been murdered on April 19th. She kept this from her mother, not wishing to worry her, for her mother had been devoted to Djon and knew nothing of Moura's involvement with Lockhart; in a letter written on her death-bed in September her mother wrote:

> My darling Mourochka – Farewell. Love Djon and take care of him and yourself. Don't be too sad for me. Life has been so very hard these last few years for me … But I will think – if, as they say, we are still able to think to the last moments – I will think of you and hope that you will be happy always. Remember me sometimes. Please, please have my body burnt. Your poor mother. I kiss you both, many times.

But in a letter to Lockhart after my father's death Moura emphasised the strain of keeping the news of his death from her sick mother:

> Here I have to go about and smile and change my black clothes so as not to let Mother guess that something has happened, before I come in to see her, to keep it all from her.

Although Moura had been actively contemplating a divorce, she wrote the following letter to Lockhart in May, immediately upon hearing the news of my father's death:

> My husband has been killed on the 19th of April. I have only heard of it the day before yesterday and the shock has been a terrible one. I am sure you will understand in what a

hopeless, endless muddle of complicated emotions I am plunged ... I don't understand your silence, Baby. For God's sake be frank with me, Baby, play fair with me as I always have and always will with you.

This was the last communication that she was to have with Lockhart for two whole years.

At the beginning of September 1919, for the first time in her life, Moura was alone. Her sister Assia, whose first husband had died of tuberculosis in 1917, had married Prince Basil Kotchoubey and was still in the Ukraine. They finally managed to escape to France in 1921 via Constantinople. Alla, her other sister, was already living in Paris with her husband. Her brother Bobik was long dead; she had now to face the fact that her reunion with Lockhart was not to happen and she stopped writing to him.

Before the revolution when she had known so many members of the British Embassy, she had met Korney Chukovsky, the official interpreter at the embassy. He had become a friend of the Benckendorffs. They used to meet him at various functions at the Anglo-Russian Club, which flourished during the First World War. Chukovsky had been a translator of English and American books into Russian and had worked as translator for the British military mission. Later he was to become Russia's most famous author of children's books, the A.A. Milne of Russia. Moura had kept in touch with him throughout this period and had heard that he was collaborating with Maxim Gorky on a publishing venture involved in the translation of English classics. She now decided to approach him in the hope of being employed as a translator. Although he didn't give her any translations to do, he understood her predicament and as a friend found enough office work for her to be able to obtain the vital identity card, which in those days served as a passport as well as a ration-card. This Moura signed in her maiden name.

Moura had worked for Chukovsky for a few weeks when, in the autumn of that year, he took her to meet Gorky, who was occupying a large apartment on Kronverskaya Prospekt. Here he had a great many people living with him, some on a permanent, others on a short-term, basis. Among them were writers, artists, family and friends. He even gave refuge in his apartment to the Grand Duke Gabriel Konstantinovich Romanov and obtained a permit for him and his wife to leave for Finland. Moura too needed both protection and work, and as she got on well with the others in the house, she was soon asked to move in with them, as had been many people whom Gorky had taken under his wing.

Alexei Maximovich Peshkov (Gorky was a pseudonym), born in 1868, 'a real man of the people' as Tolstoy had called him, had long established himself as a writer in sympathy with revolutionary ideas. His father died when he was a child and he spent his early years with his mother and grandparents. His grandmother used to read to him and had a great influence on him; when his mother died he had to find various menial jobs to keep himself alive. At the age of twenty-one he tried unsuccessfully to commit suicide, and the attempt left him with only one functioning lung. For three years he wandered like a tramp over the steppe, writing about and observing the people of his country. Then his first short story appeared in a Tiflis newspaper and gradually more essays and stories were published. In 1902 he wrote his most important play, *The Lower Depths*. It had immediate success at the Moscow Arts Theatre and soon achieved world fame.

Gorky had witnessed a great deal of evil and injustice in his wanderings through Russia and wrote about them in his autobiographical works *Childhood* and *My Universities*. His moving short story 'Birth of a Man' is about his experience of delivering a woman of her child in the open steppe. In the early days of the 1905 Revolution Gorky was active in the revolutionary movement, and he was arrested five times in his life. He lived in exile in the United States of America and in London and later, because of lung trouble, for many years on the island of Capri off Italy. In 1915 he returned to Russia and became actively involved in revolutionary work. He approved of the October Revolution of 1917 but disapproved of some of its methods. But he did not publicise his criticism, because he was anxious not to ally himself with the emigré world and with enemies of the revolution. He passionately believed in the goodness of man and his salvation through education. Even as late as 1936 when the new constitution, guaranteeing the fundamental freedom of the individual, was published on the eve of the Stalinist purges, Gorky had an almost naive faith that enabled him to write, 'Even the stones cry with joy at this achievement!'

The idea of translating the classics had been conceived by Gorky when he was still a young man. He believed that the coming of world revolution would be accelerated by the propagation on a mass scale of culture, through the publication of summaries of the literature and scientific discoveries of all nations and all ages in a simplified form, easily absorbed by the working-class reader. Translations with commentaries would be produced which would introduce workers, peasants and all young people to the masterpieces of every age from which everything superfluous and reactionary would have been expurgated. The project was to be called an encyclopaedia. The idea had matured in Gorky's mind over a period of fifteen years, but with the revolution the opportunity to implement it became actual. The first step was to found a publishing venture called Universal Literature, to undertake the translations of European and American classics on a massive scale. The charter of Universal Literature was signed in 1918 by Gorky and three close friends, I.P. Ladyzhnikov, A.N. Tikhonov and Z.I. Grzhebin. In 1919 the first three volumes were published. By providing work in this way, Gorky hoped to be able to secure the physical survival of scholars, writers and all the people who would be engaged in the project.

Gorky was at that time very much *persona grata* with the régime and was regarded as a national hero by the Russian people. He was able to save the lives of many people and give them protection from the secret police. By virtue of his friendship with Lenin, he was often able to intercede with the authorities, even though he had had differences with him about the true interpretation of the Social Democratic tradition. The relationship between Lenin and Gorky was complex. Lenin despised the old intelligentsia, but at the same time his friendship with Gorky preserved a link with them. Later on in 1921, when the great famine began, Lenin looked to Gorky to promote foreign help: he even agreed that Gorky should write to H.G. Wells and George Bernard Shaw in an effort to create an atmosphere of international goodwill towards the Soviet régime.

For Moura, moving into the big apartment on Kronverskaya marked a significant new period in her life. She had lost all that she once possessed: where she had lived in opulence she now lived near to poverty; where she had been the centre of an admiring circle, she was now having to fashion a new set of friends and a new life for herself. Divorced from her past, she was able to re-create it as she liked, and it is little surprise that so many rumours and conflicting stories gathered around her, for she herself encouraged them.

Gorky was immediately attracted to her: Moura was in need of a protector. She was by now aware of the effect that she had on men, and it was to remain her most powerful means of hanging on to what she feared she might lose. It was an attraction compounded of a vitality and an ability to make them feel that they were the most important person to her, that they alone mattered. Gorky must have been fascinated by this person from an alien world, but there was more to it than the glamour of an imperial past; the immediate physical attraction was substantiated by something deeper. Gradually, a relationship grew up between them of great warmth and intimacy; and despite the presence in the same house of Gorky's long-standing mistress, they became lovers in an affair that lasted for many years. Gorky remained devoted to her for the rest of his life. But when she first moved into his apartment she was intent on building a new life and on creating for herself the security she lacked. Having lost so much emotionally, she was determined from then on never to give up anything she acquired. Gorky admired this determination and resilience in her, the overpowering will to survive; and seen in this light, it becomes less surprising that there should have been an affair between the Gorky of *My Universities*, Lenin's friend, and the wife of an aristocrat.

But paradoxically it was Robert Bruce Lockhart who in some way had prepared Moura's mind for the new life which now began, and which was as far removed from her former existence as one could possibly have imagined. He had given her an understanding of events and a sympathy with Gorky's view of Bolshevism. Lockhart's knowledge and liberal ideas, and his understanding of Russian affairs, had stimulated and brought about in her an awareness of the social problems and injustices which had led to the rise of Bolshevism. He had shown her that it was useless to cling to the structure of society as she had known it without trying to understand the causes for its breakdown. It helped her now to fit into her new surroundings, as a novel and interesting world was opened up to her. It was a unique opportunity and with all the enthusiasm of youth she grasped it with both hands.

When Moura first moved into the apartment, however, Gorky was still living under the same roof as Maria Fyodorevna Andréeva, the famous Russian actress who had been his companion for many years, although their relationship had already broken up. She had lived and worked with him abroad during the years he had been exiled from Tsarist Russia for his part in the 1905 Revolution, first in the United States and then on the island of Capri, until he returned to Russia in 1915.

During those years Gorky's wife, Ekaterina Pavlovna Peshkova, and their son Maxim had remained in Moscow. As a young wife Ekaterina Pavlovna had been greatly upset by Gorky's association with Andréeva and they had separated. But gradually her relations with Gorky improved; they remained friends and continued to correspond and visit each other regularly. Gorky valued her opinion and remained devoted to her. By the time Moura came into his life there was little resentment on her part. Several women took pride of place at various times in Gorky's life, but Ekaterina Pavlovna returned to him when he finally went back to the Soviet Union in 1932 and they lived together in Moscow with their children and grandchildren until his death in 1936. She outlived him by thirty years and even at the age of ninety was still actively engaged in working on Gorky's archives, and to the end of her life remained at the centre of his large family.

Valentina Khodasevich, a painter and designer, who with her husband had been invited to move into Gorky's large apartment on Kronverskaya in 1919, described the communal life with Gorky in the years 1919-21.

The apartment had twelve rooms and in these lived Gorky and Maria Fyodorevna, I and my artist husband, Ivan Rakitsky, another young artist, Piotr Kriuchkov, who helped Gorky's common-law wife [M.F. Andréeva] in matters of theatre, Maria Ignatievna Benckendorff-Zakrevsky was given some secretarial work to do using her languages in the publishing group called 'Universal Literature' which Gorky had started, and finally, Mariussa Geynze, a young girl student, the daughter of an old friend of Gorky's from Nizhni Novgorod, who had come to study at the Military Academy of Medicine. In the apartment above lived Maria Andréeva's daughter with her husband as well as her nephew and his wife. Everybody foregathered for meals which made it a kind of 'commune'.

They all worked at different things, shared and pooled their rations and somehow managed to feed themselves – badly, but they survived. Meals were prepared by an energetic woman called Anna. The hours of leisure were spent together, and as they were young and in good spirits they sometimes even managed to enjoy themselves. Gorky liked this kind of ambience. Four small rooms in this apartment were allotted to him. One of these was his library, another his bedroom, the third his study, and the fourth had no furniture in it except for a few display cabinets where Gorky kept his collection of Chinese and Eastern objects. (Later, before leaving for western Europe in 1921, he gave the entire collection to the ethnographic museum.) A corner of the library was cut off by a Russian stove and Gorky had his leather chair there, where he

used to sit and work. He regarded every book as a valued
friend and treated it with love and with respect. Nobody was
allowed to take away a book from this library.

In the winter of 1919 the once magnificent city of Petrograd
was unrecognisable. Signs of death were visible everywhere.
Typhoid fever and Spanish 'flu were rampant, and dead horses
were strewn about the streets. The cold was perishing; the only
fuel available was the wood from furniture and floorboards of
the houses – often left full of gaping holes due to the destruction of doors or the breaking of windows. There was wide-
spread famine; almost no bread or cooking fats were available
in the city. Pipes remained frozen until April so that running
water was a rare luxury during those winter months. The
supply of rations came in fits and starts. Only apples would be
available at one moment, only herrings at another, sometimes
only cabbages and rotten ones at that.

These harsh conditions were aggravated by the activities of
the omnipresent officials of the Cheka who were carrying out
arbitrary arrests all over the city. Another hazard which
prevented escape was the fighting between the Reds and the
Whites in the civil war which was raging on three sides of the
city. In the west the advance of the White troops under General
Yudenich was already threatening Petrograd.

Amid this state of affairs Gorky's apartment was increasingly besieged by men and women of all classes and ages
seeking his signature of approval on applications of all kinds
to the authorities. Gorky was only too ready to sign these
papers, hoping that his intervention would be successful and
relieve the lot of a few victims of the general misery.

Friends and admirers of Gorky and Maria Andréeva would
bring along bundles of wood or planks on their backs or on
sledges, which were burned for firewood. Sometimes the
electricity supply would be cut off for several days. Then they
all gathered after dark in Ivan Rakitsky's room, which had a
fireplace where they sat by the glimmer of light. Often
Chaliapin, the world-famous bass, a friend of Gorky's youth,
and his wife would come in, both charming, imposing-looking
people, who enchanted them with songs and romances.

10 Moura in Petrograd, 1918

11 & 12 Maxim Gorky
in Sorrento

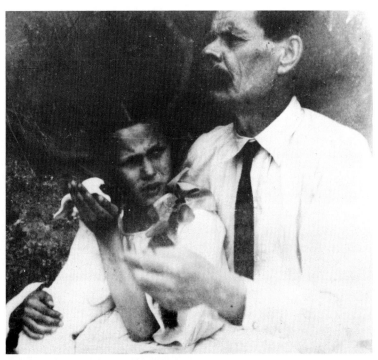

13 & 14 Gorky at villa Il Sorito with Tania and Moura in 1925

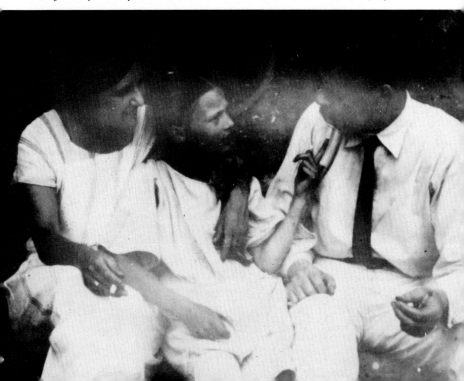

15 *Top:* Gorky pictured with his son Maxim
16 *Bottom:* H.G. Wells in discussion with Gorky on Wells's
visit to Russia

Although there was great hardship and privation everywhere in the early years of the revolution, there was also an
astonishing injection of enthusiasm into the intellectual life of
Petrograd in the early 1920s, with a great coming together of
artists and writers, fired by the same aim of providing art for
the people. The House of Art and the House of Letters were
both established at this time; and the House of Universal
Literature had already been set up. Gorky was at the centre of
this movement, for he was the foremost writer of the revolution. Many members of the intelligentsia were leaving the
country, and he was anxious to attract as many as possible of
the cream of Petrograd intelligentsia to remain and work for
their country. It was natural that the Kronverskaya apartment
became the meeting-place for them. Here Moura met, among
others, the poets Alexander Blok, Boris Pilnyak and the writers
Evgeny Zamyatin and Alexei Tolstoy.

Gorky was anxious to help everywhere he could, but particularly writers, artists and poets whose survival, in his view,
would be so necessary for the future of the Soviet Union. One
day a young poetess appeared in a state of great distress
because she was unable to breastfeed her baby, and begged
Gorky to intervene for her to receive regular supplies of milk.
He immediately wrote a letter to the department concerned. In
order to speed up things for her he implied that this request was
for his illegitimate child, but asked for this to be kept a secret!
But when other women began to turn up with the same request
and Gorky claimed all the children as his, the comrade to
whom the letters were addressed finally wrote to Gorky saying
he could no longer supply such a large number of 'Gorky
children' with milk. Everyone teased Gorky: 'You at your age
and all from different mothers – you should be ashamed of
yourself.' 'I shan't do it again, I promise,' he laughed.

In the 1920s there was a passionate interest in education in
the Soviet Union. Gorky knew that H.G. Wells was fired by the
same desire to bring art and literature to the common people.
That was the guiding force behind his own endeavours.
Moreover, the Soviet leadership was aware that it needed as
many foreign friends as possible. Gorky persuaded Lenin that

Wells was a man whose opinion would command respect on both sides of the Atlantic. Accordingly Gorky invited Wells to stay with him in Petrograd to see at first hand the work that had been done in the field of popular education, and the reforms brought about by the revolution. Wells arrived in Petrograd in September 1920 with his son Gip, a young scientist. They were given the room which had been occupied by Moura and the student, Mariussa (the two youngest members of the group). Moura was moved on to a mattress in Rakitsky's room and Mariussa on to a spare bed with Mme Khodasevich and her husband. Mme Khodasevich was given the task of entertaining Gip, with whom she was able to converse in French. As Gip was then a student of zoology she took him to the zoo, where he was particularly amused by the elephant, which had been taught to receive paper money from visitors and then hand the notes to the keeper in return for food. He was quite able to distinguish paper money from ordinary paper, which he would drop. Gip was of course also shown all the other sights of the city. Wells himself was very lively and interested. In his long talks with Gorky, Moura was often called in to interpret. In the recently published third volume of his autobiography, *H.G. Wells in Love*, Wells, referring to this first meeting, writes:

> She was wearing an old khaki British army waterproof and a shabby black dress; her only hat was some twisted-up piece of black – a stocking, I think – and yet she had magnificence. She stuck her hands in the pockets of her waterproof, and seemed not simply to brave the world but disposed to order it about.
>
> She was now my official interpreter. And she presented herself to my eyes as gallant, unbroken and adorable. I fell in love with her, made love to her, and one night at my entreaty she flitted noiselessly through the crowded apartments in Gorky's flat to my embraces.

Moura's relationship with Wells, which started with his journey to Petrograd in 1920, was to prove in later years of vital importance to them both. But at this time it represents more her constant desire to acquire and to extend her power over other men. She remained in her way devoted to Gorky for the rest of his life; and typically she was less than truthful with Wells about the past, even inventing a meeting with him six years previously at a house I know she never visited. She also told him she had been married twice before. But no matter how much mystery she created, she successfully established an emotional hold on H.G. Wells in that week.

By the end of 1920, however, the secure life that Moura had built for herself on Kronverskaya came under threat. Ever since his attempted suicide, Gorky's health had been frail, and it was becoming increasingly important that he should be moved out of Russia to a warmer climate. Lenin at one time had been only too keen to have Gorky identify himself with the aims of the régime. They had, however, had a number of differences and Lenin, though genuinely concerned for Gorky's health, was keen for him to be out of the country for a while. He now urged him to go abroad for the treatment of his lungs. The pressure on Gorky to leave increased through the winter of 1920, and although at first he would not hear of it, it was evident that he would not be able to stay in Russia much longer.

Moura was clearly worried: it would be dangerous for her to be left behind in Russia without Gorky's protection. By December it was decided that her only course of action was to leave Russia clandestinely.

There was a recognised escape route from Russia to Estonia across the ice-bound river Narova. There were experienced guides who received a handsome fee for escorting people out of Russia, and the frontier guards, fully aware of the regular traffic, made only desultory attempts to intercept the flow of refugees. With a small group of four people, Moura attempted what should have been a fairly straightforward walk over the ice one night in December 1920. But by ill luck they had chosen a night when the Soviet border patrol was more alert than usual. Moura and her four companions were detected and arrested.

Moura herself used to tell the story that as she and her companions were being marched off to the Gorohavaya prison by the border patrol, they passed within sight of her former house; and the cook, seeing her in the hands of the police, immediately realised what had happened and telephoned Gorky. This is probably just a fanciful story on my mother's part; but it is certainly true that she somehow managed to contact Gorky, the one man in Russia who could help her, and explain her plight. There was only one sure way for Gorky to secure her release and that was to approach Dzerzhinsky, then head of the Cheka. By good fortune Dzerzhinsky was a close friend of Ekaterina Pavlovna, and ironically it was she who helped to intercede on Moura's behalf. Moura was quickly released and returned to Gorky's apartment. But plans for Gorky's departure were by now well advanced, and realising that Moura had to leave before him, Gorky prevailed on Djerzhinsky to issue her with an exit visa to visit her children in Estonia. Estonia was now an independent state and traffic with the Soviet Union was gradually beginning to be established. In the spring of 1921 the papers came through and my mother left to rejoin the family she had not seen for more than three years.

Gorky's disagreement with Lenin and his rapidly failing health meant that he could not survive another winter in Petrograd. In the spring of that same year he sent Maria Andréeva, his son Maxim and Piotr Kriuchkov, now his personal secretary, to Berlin as the advance party to prepare somewhere for him to stay until a place of asylum with a suitable climate for his lung trouble could be found. In October 1921 Gorky finally left Russia; the 'commune' on Kronverskaya which had been a place of such hope and common purpose broke up. His friends realised that it was the end of an era when a droshky drove him to the Finland Station in Petrograd from where a train took him to Helsinki on his way to Germany.

Throughout this period we had no contact with Moura at all. She only becomes a real person for me when she turns up in Kallijärv in May 1921.

CHAPTER VII
Moura's Return

We had not seen my mother since the spring of 1918 and were barely able to remember her. I had wondered about the reasons for her absence over the years, but had had only rumours to go on. My first vivid memory of her is when I was six years old. A room was being prepared for her and there was a general atmosphere of anticipation and excitement in the house. I was aware that Aunt Cossé did not share the general sense of excitement, but Micky, as the time approached, was in a state of growing exhilaration. I was later to find out that before the arrival of any member of our family Micky would always become very moody, fluctuating between happiness and tetchy irritability, perhaps because she was aware that such visits could only be brief. However, we children were infected by Micky's increasing excitement, although we had no idea what to expect.

I can remember wondering what my mother would be like, but I have no memory of her actual arrival at Kallijärv. She must have come at night after we had gone to bed. But on the morning after her arrival Micky took us to meet her, as far as I was concerned for the first time. It is curious, when I think of it now, that the moment was so unemotional. I have a very clear picture of the room and of a woman sitting up in bed. I remember thinking that she was larger than I had expected and that this rather healthy-looking person did not correspond to the stories of hunger and privation we had been told.

But I was also aware that this woman was a total stranger and I felt at that first meeting nothing of what one might expect. I suspect, looking back on it, that there was a great deal of embarrassment on both sides which prevented any closeness between us straight away. Micky, while fussing around Moura, very soon ushered us out of the room again, telling us that she must be left to rest as she was very tired. That was my first real meeting with my mother and yet it is remarkable only for its ordinariness.

For all the time I knew her Moura never got up before lunchtime, telephoning, answering letters and receiving the odd caller in her bedroom, and certainly for that week I think that she remained in bed more or less the whole time. It is true that she had gone through a series of great ordeals and must have been exhausted, both physically and emotionally. But it was also true that she expected members of the family to pay court to her throughout the day. They would all be summoned one by one to her bedside as she wanted them. There was an aura of mystery about why and where she had been all this time, and I suppose, thinking back now, that it was because everyone disapproved of her prolonged absence and her association with those who were considered by my uncles and aunts to be enemies of their country.

The Baltic families in Estonia had completely closed minds about the Bolsheviks. They could not accept them as the legitimate government of Russia and they could not believe that the Communist régime would survive for any considerable period. As members of the former governing class, they had believed in the autocratic régime of the Tsar as if it were a religion. They regarded the Communist régime which had murdered the Tsar as a criminal conspiracy with which no civilised person should have any dealings. They were reinforced in their attitude by the fact that most of them had suffered personally at the hands of the Bolsheviks, losing all their possessions and in many cases their close relatives or intimate friends. Many of them dreamed of the eventual reestablishment of the Tsarist régime which would restore them to their positions and estates.

It was inevitable that people who firmly held these beliefs should be suspicious of Moura and that they should want to have some answers about her activities during the past three years. During all this time there had been virtually no communication between her and her relatives and, when she arrived in Estonia, both the Benckendorff side of the family, who had taken charge of us 'orphans', and the Estonian authorities regarded her with the deepest suspicion. The governments of the independent Baltic States were nervous of the Soviet Union anyway. As Moura had lost her right to apply for Estonian citizenship by staying on in Petrograd after 1918, the Estonians were sceptical about her motives for visiting the country, and as a Soviet citizen would grant her only a permit to stay in the country for three months to visit us after which she would have to return to Russia. Her in-laws at first would not let her see her children, not until they had heard her story.

Why had she not moved her mother to her country home in Estonia via Finland when it was still possible? Why had she gone back to Russia? Why had she not stayed in Estonia with her husband and children? What was the truth about her relationship with the Communists?

There was a strange custom among the Baltic nobility, who had established a court of honour (*Ehrengericht*) – a relic of past ages – to review, and censure when necessary, breaches of their code of ethics. The elected head of the Baltic nobility at the time was Count Ignatiev. He convened a court of honour to review Moura's connections with the Communist régime in Russia, to which Moura was summoned. After detailed questioning it was finally declared that she had not been guilty of collaboration with the Bolsheviks. I do not think there is any record of the proceedings or of Moura's defence against the accusations. But although she was 'cleared', some of the Balts retained their suspicions and it was only with the passage of time that her story – that she had remained in Petrograd to be with her sick mother, and that it had been impossible for her to leave once the frontier between Russia and Estonia had been closed – was reluctantly accepted. Only her closest friends knew of her involvement with Bruce Lockhart. That is why the publication of *Memoirs of a British Agent*, in which Lockhart describes his romance with Moura in Moscow in 1918, came as such a great shock to her relatives.

We children inevitably heard snippets of the endless discussions which were aroused by all these matters. I remember hearing Micky say that Moura had caught lice while she was in a prison in Moscow and that they had settled under the skin of her arms. After hearing this I would, every time I was taken to see her, stare at her arms to see if I could discover any of these lice, which of course I never did. I asked Micky why Moura had been arrested, but she brushed it off with, 'That's all finished and done with – it wasn't for long', and I asked no more questions and forgot about it.

Everyone around us had been through great hardships, which we had heard about throughout our childhood. We were therefore not unduly impressed by new stories of lack of food, of prison, and of escapes. But we were puzzled and impressed by the fact that the behaviour of the adults around us gave Moura an air of mystery. Somehow we were left with the impression that she must have been involved in something wicked and unmentionable, for we were always in some sense aware that the adults were trying to protect us from a world and a set of values of which they strongly disapproved, but which we really did not understand at all and which therefore seemed even more fascinating.

I remember an incident soon after Moura's return – I must have been about seven – which supported this impression. Every year, we used to attend the Easter services at the Russian Orthodox Church. That particular year Moura had come to church with us. But when we all went to Communion she stayed at the back of the church 'Could she have murdered someone or taken part in a robbery?' I wondered. That would explain it. But I felt that whatever it was I would protect her, and I remember walking back from the altar to where she stood and stroking her lovely soft fur coat to reassure her that I was on her side. She knew nothing of these thoughts, of course, and merely smiled at me. But I felt for the first time a closeness to my mother and an affection that I had not known before.

After a short period of rest in Kallijärv, Moura spent the middle of most weeks in Tallinn, the capital of Estonia, and we resumed our normal life with daily school work. Baron and Baroness Bengt Stackelberg, who had been friends of the Benckendorffs since Petersburg days, gave her a room in their flat in Tallinn. So many things had to be sorted out and explained. Gradually, but only much later, they fell into place for me.

But Moura's situation was still pretty desperate. Gorky's son and daughter-in-law were already in Germany preparing for his arrival in the west. Moura managed to get in touch with them and to tell them of the difficulties she had had on reaching Estonia. At Gorky's request a sum of money was transferred to her from Germany. But it was not only money that she needed. In order to be able to move about freely she had to have a passport. She had waited for Bruce Lockhart for three years, and she knew now that he never intended to make his life with her. She consulted a lawyer in Estonia and was persuaded by him that the best solution for her would be to marry an Estonian subject in order to obtain Estonian citizenship. He introduced her to Baron Nicolai Budberg.

The Budbergs were another of the landowning Baltic families. Nicolai Budberg was educated in the traditional fashion at the Military Staff College in St Petersburg. After the revolution he remained in Estonia when the country achieved its independence. Without any civilian professional training he lapsed into a life of pleasure and relied on gambling to provide him with the funds necessary to live.

At the time when Lai was introduced to Moura he was in a very awkward situation. An inveterate gambler at cards, he had incurred enormous debts and was being pressurised to leave the country. But first he would be obliged to pay his debts. In return for a marriage ceremony, Moura was to pay them out of a sum of money which Gorky's financial manager had sent her from Germany. Then together they would leave for Berlin. Since German was Budberg's second language Berlin was an obvious place to go to, and it would also suit Moura to be nearer to Gorky, whose arrival in the west was now imminent. But the future of her relationship with Gorky was uncertain. There had been the beginning of an intimate relationship, but would it continue on a permanent basis when they met again outside Russia? She was not sure. There were rumours that Gorky had resumed his relationship with the wife of the writer A.N. Tikhonov. If this was true, the affair did not last long, but it was enough to make Moura feel even less secure.

At the end of October 1921 Moura went from Estonia to see Gorky in Finland on his way from Russia to Germany. She told him that she intended to marry a certain Baron Budberg. Gorky wrote at the time to a friend:

> In Finland I saw Maria Ignatievna. She is slimmer and has generally become somewhat nicer – and, as formerly, knows and is interested in everything. An excellent person. She tells me that she intends to marry some kind of a baron, but we all protest with energy – let the baron find himself some other object of his fancy – this one is one of us!

But marry Budberg she did only two weeks later, although she did not write to tell Gorky of the event until a month afterwards.

When Paul and I were told of Moura's forthcoming wedding we packed our bags and walked out into the woods to leave home. Needless to say , we did not get very far. I don't know why we disliked the idea so much. We hardly knew Budberg, but I do remember thinking that he was ugly and had a bald, egg-shaped head; and of course we sensed that our close relations, and especially Micky, thoroughly disapproved of the marriage.

Of the marriage service itself, in the Russian Orthodox Church in November 1921 in Tallinn, I have only a hazy memory. At the church it was a sad spectacle – all the aunts and relations spent their time weeping, which was puzzling for a child of seven. It was a large social function, but I suspect that most of those present were aware that the motives behind the match were more pragmatic than passionate. Certainly it must have felt strange welcoming back into respectable Baltic society somebody who had so recently been brought before the *Ehrengericht*. It is of course not unusual for people to weep at weddings, and I remember being puzzled that what should have been a happy and joyous occasion was marked in the church by the expressed sadness on the faces of my relations.

They cannot have failed to be aware of the sharp contrast between the wedding of my mother and father in St Petersburg some ten years previously and this one. The first was apparently a perfect match full of so many bright hopes for the future, while the second was so obviously a marriage of convenience to a man who had gambled away his inheritance. I did not realize any of this at the time. All I knew was that everyone appeared rather gloomy in the church.

But the atmosphere changed at the wedding lunch, which was a marvellous occasion held in the Club of the Nobility, as it was called. A long table had been set up in the splendid hall, at which all the guests sat. By now everyone had given up crying and was enjoying themselves. I can still remember the crisp white tablecloth and the waiters dressed in black suits with white gloves serving us with delicious dishes, the like of which I had never seen before. Neither had I ever seen a waiter nor even been waited on, and I was reported to have asked my Uncle Sasha Benckendorff, 'Why do some of the gentlemen serve and others sit at the table?' Years later, when he disapproved of what he called my Socialist views, he used to say that he might have foreseen them, as already then I had shown signs of wishing for equality among men.

After their marriage Moura and Lai remained in Tallinn for a few weeks prior to their departure for Berlin. They were immediately accepted in the round of parties. The Baltic society of Tallinn represented a curious paradox: while obsessed by notions of honour and the feudal traditions exemplified by the *Ritterschaft* which the Balts had brought with them, they were now a ruling class with nobody and nothing to rule, landowners stripped of their lands. And so, running alongside their exaggerated sense of honour was a feeling of dissipation, a feeling that so often occurs when a society has lost its central reason for existence. In contrast to the outward appearances of Baltic society, this was a world of too much drinking and easy promiscuity. The prevalent mood was one of *après nous le déluge*. I heard of this years later from my Uncle Sasha, who had been part of the same circle in that period, intent only on having a good time.

Early in 1922 Moura and Budberg left for Berlin. It was presumably Moura's plan to be near Gorky and at the same time to be in a city where a divorce could more easily be arranged than in Estonia. The family had, it seems, accepted that Moura would not stay in Kallijärv and, already used to her absence, we children took it for granted that she had to go. It seemed reasonable too that she and Lai would be more likely to find work abroad. Her work, we were later told, was to become secretary to Maxim Gorky. By the autumn of 1922 Lai Budberg had left Europe to live in South America, where he was said to have kept his head above water by giving bridge lessons. Their divorce was pronounced in December 1926 by a Berlin court in the absence of both parties. Budberg later married again and died in Rio de Janeiro in 1972.

CHAPTER VIII

Sorrento

Gorky, in the meantime, had settled temporarily with nearly all the same members of his Petrograd community of friends in Heringsdorf, a small seaside resort on the Baltic. His health was improving and he was getting stronger. With him were also his son Maxim and Maxim's newly acquired beautiful wife Nadezhda. Maxim Peshkov was a gifted and versatile young man. He lived with, and worked as secretary and interpreter for, his father from 1921 to the time of his sudden death in Moscow in 1934. He spoke several European languages fluently, was a talented cartoonist and had a delightful gift for writing light poetry. He was high-spirited and easygoing. Yet it could not have been easy to be the son of Maxim

1. Maxim's imaginative drawing and Russo-German poem for Tania.

Gorky. His father adored him and provided for him in every way, so that he had never had to struggle for anything. Despite his obvious gifts, there was always a trace of immaturity in him. But his father's protective love and care was loyally repaid by both Maxim and Nadejda in Sorrento and later in Russia.

Gorky's close relationship with Maria Fyodorevna Andréeva had come to an end even before he left Russia in 1921. She had been appointed personally by Lenin as the official representative of the Soviet Government based in Berlin to raise funds in Europe and America to meet the distress caused by the famine in Russia. Later, in 1924, she returned to the Soviet Union having been offered the important post as head of the government organisation responsible for the theatre. And so by 1922 the way was clear for Moura to join Gorky in his establishment in Germany.

She was not yet thirty. My father was dead. The marriage to Budberg had served its purpose. Gorky had made it clear that he wanted her as his permanent companion and that he would provide financial support for her children. She was herself clearly very drawn towards him. And yet she did not decide to join him in Germany straight away.

After her marriage to Budberg she had written to Gorky telling him of the event. The reasons she gave him were plausible but not strictly truthful. As always, her letters were carefully thought out and designed to give the image she wanted to present of herself, often distorting the truth. She was holding Gorky at bay while she continued to say that she would soon be with him, but that she had family problems and had been seriously ill. In reality she was postponing her decision. I believe that the reason she would not commit herself was not her marriage to Budberg so much as the hope that Lockhart would contact her and arrange a meeting which would lead to some kind of continuation of their relationship. She had written her letter of farewell to him in June, a month after her arrival in Estonia, and although it appeared to be final, she was still hoping that he would respond. However, by the beginning of 1922 she realised that his silence meant that her future and security would never lie with him, and it was only in May, when Gorky moved to Heringsdorf, that she finally went to live with him.

In the crowded apartment in Petrograd there had not been much chance for Moura and Gorky to be alone together. But in Heringsdorf and later in Saarov, a resort east of Berlin to which Gorky and his entourage moved, they had their own separate quarters where they lived together. As Gorky's partner, she now presided with him over the rest of his household.

Saarov was a lonely and soulless place and Gorky was now a very sick man. His health was always precarious, but he had resigned himself to it and was able to bury himself in his writing. From time to time writers and artists would come for short visits to talk and to pay homage to the great man. Among them were the writers Vladislav Khodasevich, Andrey Bely, Isaak Babel, Alexei Tolstoy and a number of other emigré intellectuals. As the pre-eminent Soviet writer and a friend of Lenin, Gorky's opinion was eagerly sought by writers and artists who had yet to decide whether or not to commit themselves to the new revolutionary state. In the summer of 1923 Gorky moved to Güntersthal near Freiburg, in south-west Germany. This was a more attractive town and he found the local inhabitants more agreeable than the Prussians. When he was a little better, he was able to work ten hours a day. It was at that time that he also started a bi-monthly literary magazine in Russian, *Beseda*, which was to be published in Berlin, but its circulation was aimed at Soviet Russia with contributions from Soviet as well as emigré writers.

The Soviet authorities took a long time to give the go-ahead. Meanwhile Gorky invited contributions from writers from all over Europe, including H.G. Wells, Galsworthy, Stefan Zweig and Romain Rolland. He became more and more impatient and threatened to begin writing for Russian emigré papers if permission was not granted to circulate his journal in the Soviet Union. This threat he never carried out. Finally he decided to go ahead without waiting for Soviet approval, and to publish the first issue. It included an article by Galsworthy lamenting the declining state of literature in western Europe since the First World War. But the necessary permission to circulate *Beseda* in the Soviet Union never came, and deprived of this outlet it had no future. Lenin died while negotiations were still going on, and it became even less likely now that Gorky's hope would come true. To his great disappointment the journal never took off.

In 1924, after three years of unsettled existence in different parts of Germany and a short period in Czechoslovakia, Gorky was invited by the Italian Government to settle permanently in Italy, for the sake of his health. In doing this, the Italian Government repeated the hospitality which they had given him after the 1905 Revolution, when he had spent several years on Capri. Gorky was delighted, and he and all those living with him – now including Moura – moved to Sorrento, south of Naples, into a large villa, Il Sorito. It belonged to an Italian duke who himself lived in Naples, and was prepared to let the villa on condition that his two unmarried daughters remained in a wing of the house where they occupied two large rooms and a balcony, and had their own separate entrance. The villa stood to the west of Sorrento on a promontory. To the north stretched the whole panorama of the Bay of Naples. To the south were hills, and to the west across the water lay the island of Capri.

Il Sorito was an enchanting property: the villa was large enough to accommodate all Gorky's family and friends, and there was a spacious garden with cypress trees and a tennis court. Gorky was extremely happy there and the climate suited him. His room had a view over the Bay of Naples and Mount Vesuvius. He was deeply moved by the beauty of the landscape every time he looked out, and proudly showed it to his many visitors. He would often go to Naples where the local people loved and admired him. People would recognise him in the street and rush up to grab his hands. If he took refuge by getting into a horse-drawn carriage they would surround the carriage shouting, 'Viva Gorky! Caríno!' and some of them would jump on to the step to touch their beloved illustríssimo. He would spend hours in the art gallery in Naples and knew every famous work in it.

In Il Sorito, Gorky held open house for Russian intellectuals. These included both emigré and Soviet authors, singers and artists who sought his advice and at the same time brought him news from his country. Many writers from western European countries were also frequent visitors. They were usually put up in a hotel called Minerva opposite his villa. Some would stay for a few days, others for weeks or even months. In fact people lived in Gorky's house in Sorrento rather like they used to live in country houses before the revolution in Russia.

It was Gorky's custom to work long hours, but in the evenings he had time for each one of those who met at the villa for dinner, music and conversation. Moura was by now established as mistress of the house. When she was away Gorky's daughter-in-law, Nadezhda Alexéevna, was in charge. Moura or Gorky's son Maxim also interpreted for Italian, German and French visitors as Gorky himself spoke no foreign languages. The villa was a place where men of talent often came together. The atmosphere was relaxed, and every member of the colony had his own work to do. But there was also time for play and enjoyment: there was tennis, and there were walks, for exercise. In summer the climate was conducive to a general desire for *dolce far niente*, and in the evenings everyone would foregather on the large terrace outside Gorky's room and talk, drink wine and make or listen to music.

Twice a year Moura left Sorrento to visit us at Kallijärv, in winter for a short, and in summer for a longer, visit. In 1925 Gorky invited her to bring me, my brother Paul and our cousin Kira, together with Micky, to spend the summer months in Sorrento with him. I was then ten years old. We had never been 'abroad' and our excitement was great, especially as Micky was to come with us. I remember a long and stuffy train journey which left me exhausted by the time our party, with Micky in charge, reached Rome, where Moura met us. It was on a hot afternoon in July that we arrived in Sorrento and were installed in the Hotel Minerva opposite Il Sorito. That evening we were taken across to meet Gorky and all the inhabitants of his villa. Of my first meeting with Gorky I remember few details, but I have a strong recollection of what seemed an immensely tall man who, although not heavily built, gave a feeling of great strength; but who was not at all forbidding, even to a nervous ten-year-old, because of his extraordinarily kind eyes. Those and his funny drooping moustache put me immediately at my ease. My recollections of him over the summer are of a slightly stooping, snub-nosed figure who often wore an embroidered Tatar skull cap. His voice was very deep. He always seemed in poor health and troubled by a cough, especially after taking part in our games and walks. He was very fond of music: I remember seeing him one evening so moved by the song of a visiting singer friend that it brought tears to his eyes.

Children then were not aware of the physical relationships between grown-ups; it never occurred to me at the time that his relationship with my mother was different from that with the rest of the household. I did not then distinguish between shades of friendships, or wonder about them. He seemed to me to treat everybody with the same kindness and consideration. We felt at home at once: Gorky had a special way with children.

Valentina Khodasevich, the painter and theatre designer who had been a member of Gorky's 'commune' in Petrograd, and a close friend, was now spending long periods at Il Sorito, until at the end of 1925 she returned to Russia to work at the Maryinsky Theatre. In her memoirs, remembering the summer of 1925 spent in Sorrento, she wrote:

Moura – by now Budberg – periodically disappeared to visit her children in Estonia. But in the summer of 1925 Gorky suggested that she bring her children and their old English governess to Sorrento. The youngest, Tania (very like her mother), is ten years old, her brother Paul is eleven and their cousin Kira is sixteen. The children are well cared for, nice-looking and high spirited. Alexei Maximovich was glad to see that they actually existed! Their arrival rather changed his hermit-like existence. He even used to take part in the games in the evenings which the children taught us all. Their favourite game was called 'Kids'. We were all of us 'kids'. Tania was the goat. At her piercing cry: 'Kids, kids, the wolf is here!' we all raced across the yard in front of the house towards her while Paul, the wolf, rushed out to catch us. The one whom he managed to catch before getting 'home' became the next 'wolf'. This was repeated and repeated until Gorky began to cough and became breathless. But Tania was quite tireless and quite merciless with him. The other game was less exhausting and was called 'Napoleon's tomb'. Tanya and Paul placed a bowl with water and a sponge under a table which they covered with a cloth which reached down to the ground. They crouched under this table and called in a threatening voice: 'This is Napoleon's tomb. A frightening place! Come and see for yourself!' The inquisitive and unsuspecting person who came to look would have a wet sponge wiped over his face and water poured down his neck. The children thought this the most amusing of all games and laughed uproariously. It amused us all greatly and Gorky laughed and was quite prepared to look into the 'tomb of Napoleon' several times in succession.

But all these games of an evening made his cough worse and also brought on his asthma. So in the end the doctor forbade him to take part in them.

For me it was a wonderful and memorable summer. It was also almost the first time that I can remember being fully aware of Moura as my mother. She seemed happier and more relaxed. Strangely, I think that this was largely due to Gorky. I believe that he thought it wrong that we should be separated completely from our mother. He enjoyed having us around, played games with us every day and was amused by us, and in this way Moura was included too, and gave us more of her time. She was not naturally good with young children. In Kallijärv we were always left much more to our own devices, but here in Sorrento, although she did not take part in our games, we felt she was much more involved with us. It was also

of course the first time that we had been in her presence for a
period as long as two whole months.

During the day we went for walks, we bathed in the sea. To
get to the sea we walked through a lemon grove and sometimes
we were allowed to pick a lemon off the trees. We ate delicious
meals and every kind of wonderful fruit we had never seen
before – fresh figs, peaches and bananas. We watched the
grown-ups play tennis and were ball-boys for them. The cool
evenings were the highlight of the day, when Gorky stopped
work at about five o'clock and the entire household joined him
in the garden or on the terrace. I remember those games
Valentina Khodasevich describes so well. We seemed to play
them every night. The entire household took part in them:
Gorky, his son Maxim, his daughter-in-law Nadezhda,
Rakitsky the painter, Ramsha the bassoonist, Valentina
Khodasevich, and every one of them was not only friendly and
infinitely kind, but also appeared to be amused and delighted
by us. We felt this atmosphere of affection towards us and we
thrived on it, and sensed at once Gorky's renowned love of
children. I think I must have been quite a pest at times, for I
wouldn't leave his side when he was around, but he always
made me feel that I was special.

During the first few years that followed my father's death,
right up to the year we went to Sorrento, we had really lived a
very isolated and almost lonely existence in Kallijärv, with
Micky and Aunt Cossé for adult company. Life was simple
with few luxuries, and the difficulties of transport made
communication with and visits to other estates very rare. We
children were lucky to have each other as we were left very
much to our own amusements.

In Sorrento we were the only children among ten or more
adults making up Gorky's family and friends. But they always
seemed to have time for us, whether it was playing games or
including us in every activity, even the music and talk during
the long summer evenings. Treated as we were, almost as
adults, I remember the excitement and stimulation of hearing
for the first time so many artistic things discussed and
appreciated.

At ten a child may 'know' certain things without fully understanding them. I remember 'knowing' that Gorky was said to be an atheist, which meant he did not believe in God. It worried me because I had never before met anyone who did not. But one day when Gorky, Moura, my brother and I were walking somewhere – where it was I can't remember – we came across a little church which he thought a beautiful building, and when Paul and I started to fight and chase one another, Gorky said to us, 'No, not here. You may offend and hurt some people. It is never good to do that.' I remember this, because even at ten I felt that here was a kind and a good man, and wondered why it had been said in my hearing in a disparaging way that he 'didn't believe in God'. Maybe, I thought, one did not have to believe in God after all.

I remember too sitting for my portrait, which Gorky had asked Valentina Khodasevich to paint for him. At the time I had a round face and two long dark plaits, and I was very proud that Gorky wanted to have me painted and sat still for longish periods. 'I was very fond of Tania,' writes Valentina Khodasevich in her memoirs. 'I painted her portrait for Alexei Maximovich but, as always, I was not satisfied with it and showed it to no one.' The portrait was finished before we left Sorrento, but when we asked the Peshkovs years later what had happened to it, they thought it must have got lost when Gorky left Sorrento. Unfortunately, I was unable to ask Valentina Khodasevich about it when I myself was visiting Russia just before her death in 1970.

I also remember, maybe wrongly, that during the day Gorky was always at work, while the rest of the large household seemed to spend a great deal of time sitting in the sun, talking, occasionally playing tennis, but generally not seeming to me to be very busy. It was as if they were waiting for the great man to emerge, when life would become animated again.

We spent two months in Sorrento. Just before we were due to return to Estonia, a trip to Capri was arranged for our benefit. I remember swimming in the Grotto, and feeling very proud because we children, having been brought up by the lake in Kallijärv, were good swimmers, while no one else in the party could swim at all. I remember listening to the echo and wondering at the blueness of the water. I remember the feeling of great sadness that it was our last day. It seemed to me that I had known everybody here for ever and I had grown to love each one of them.

Moura was going to take us as far as Berlin and then return to Sorrento. But in Berlin my brother Paul developed an infected appendix and had to undergo an emergency operation. Micky moved into hospital with him, and my cousin Kira and I were parked in a small hotel where we were left more or less to our own devices. The adults were too worried about Paul to give Kira and me their attention. I remember little of Berlin itself, as we were too young to venture very far on our own. We seem to have spent a lot of time in the hotel. I had never seen a mechanical lift before and we rode up and down, delighted to take the other guests to their floors all day. There were also the wonderful meals which we ordered ourselves, especially quantities of a fruit dessert we loved. Moura had left us as soon as Paul's operation was successfully over. When he had recovered sufficiently to travel, Micky took us by train back to Estonia, back to our lessons and home routine. But there was the excitement of our new cousin, Nathalie – Aunt Zoria's second child, who had been born just before we left and who we discovered had become quite a character while we were away.

As I look back on it now, I remember in particular the warm feeling of happiness which permeated the household of Maxim Gorky that summer, and I recall vividly my childhood love and affection for him. There was something so human and even touching about this huge, gruff man. I thought him quite wonderful, serious and gay, gentle with us children and compassionate to everybody. I still have a little Dresden figure of a child and a wolf which he gave me, and a lovely emerald cross which I cherish. But something I cherished more than anything at the time were a few lines which he wrote in his very distinctive handwriting in a little album I used to have where friends and school-fellows wrote either a short poem or a few words to be remembered by:

2. Gorky's handwritten note to Tania.

'You are a very dear person, Tania, I shall be lonely without you for I have grown to love you. Alexei Maximovich.'

This was the year 1925. I never saw Gorky again. But I have carried with me throughout my life the profound emotional effect of the two months I spent in Sorrento. Although I was only ten years old, Gorky's warmth and humanity made a deep impression on me that predisposed me, when I came to think things through for myself and to discuss them with my own friends, towards Russian Communism and away from German Fascism, a movement which was gaining much support among the Baltic community in Estonia as I grew up.

Disillusionment came later for me when the truth became known about the brutal repression of the Stalinist régime in Russia; but for many years it seemed to me that the Socialist ideals of Russia offered the best chance of social and political justice for the country. If the leaders in Russia were like Gorky and thought like him – this self-taught man who had fought so hard for a new Russia – then I felt that there must be much that was good in Communism.

CHAPTER IX
Kallijärv

After our return from Sorrento in 1925, life in Kallijärv began
to open up. It became a meeting-place for relatives, friends and
visitors of all ages and a variety of nationalities – the lively,
enchanting place I remember. A number of factors no doubt
contributed to this: I was growing up and was taking more
notice of what people were saying and thinking; Moura's visits
became more frequent and she attracted her own friends to
visit Kallijärv; and perhaps most important as far as I was
concerned, Aunt Cossé had left and the house was now in the
charge of Uncle Sasha and his wife Zoria who came to live with
us. Also, as we children grew older we went away to school,
returning only for holidays to Kallijärv, which we loved
already, but which now seemed all the more precious and
special. Certainly I look back on it as the most important
influence on me at that time. In order to understand my story it
is necessary to know what the atmosphere there was like
between 1925 and 1939, when I last saw Kallijärv just before
the outbreak of the Second World War.

Our house was quite unlike the homes of our Baltic relations
whom we occasionally visited. As a child, I felt this very
strongly. But if asked what was the special quality of the
atmosphere of Kallijärv, I would find it hard to pin down. It
was not only the romantic setting by a lake flanked by a forest.

One feature of our household was that it was more Russian
than Baltic in character, and its members probably had wider
interests than those of other Baltic households in Estonia.
Moura, Zoria, Moussia Stackelberg, a close family friend who
with her family regularly spent every summer in a cottage on
our estate, were all three Russian women of aristocratic birth
who had married into the Baltic nobility. Their husbands and
their ancestors had been very much part of the administration

of the Russian empire, and felt themselves deeply attached to Tsarist Russia. Their outlook was therefore wider and different from that of some Baltic families who had kept closer to their German origins. I suspect this was partly because the Russian language was spoken and Russian literature was read in their houses, and as a result there was an extra viewpoint. Certainly this was true with regard to world affairs. Although they were committedly anti-Communist, unlike many of the Baltic nobility they were equally fiercely anti-Fascist and were utterly opposed to Hitler's rise to power. After the forced exodus of the Balts from Estonia in 1939 and the subsequent German invasion of Russia, my Uncle Sasha – as a Russian speaker – was called up to interpret in the German army. He saw this service, however naively, as a means of returning to Russia and helping to defeat the Communists and restoring Russia to its former glory, rather than as a means of helping Hitler. However misjudged this may have appeared to me at the time, he apparently earned the devotion of the native population of Minsk where he was appointed town major, because he saw himself as a compatriot rather than as a representative of a conquering army.

While the Russian aristocracy suffered the loss of homes, land, position and influence as a result of the revolution, the Baltic families with estates in Estonia had, on the whole, been allowed to remain in their own homes on their estates, although their land had been confiscated, with the result that for the Baltic families with close Russian connections the upheaval had been far greater. Another distinguishing characteristic was that the Russian wives of the Balts in our family had retained their Russian Orthodox faith, and although their husbands had officially remained Lutheran, they had in many cases become so Russified that they too tended to worship at the Orthodox services.

Ours was essentially a matriarchal household where the strong-minded Russian women were in charge and interested in everything. As was the case in many Baltic households, most of the menfolk had been killed in the revolution or in the civil war which followed. Those who had survived and lived in

Estonia found work in the town during the week and were only at home for weekends and holidays. Hospitality had always been part of their way of life and they continued to practise it in Estonia.

Arguments at Kallijärv, especially in the 1930s when I was already in my teens, were endless and sometimes heated – about religion, politics, behaviour; and visitors, young and old, found themselves drawn into these at once. But they were friendly arguments and the very air was saturated with affectionate interest in people. There was an intellectual gaiety, almost poetic, about it all. After a few days of adapting themselves to the household, most people seemed to become kinder, more interesting and more gentle. There was a general lack of tension, very few rules, few organised activities. In summer there was a constant coming and going, but there was never a fuss about domestic arrangements. These were made quickly behind the scenes with only one aim, to make welcome and accommodate any number of guests. Grown-ups and children set to at once to make this possible.

Meals were the only occasions for which we had to be on time. Food was simple and by that time there was plenty of it. If a casserole had been prepared by Leeni for twelve and more people had turned up, potatoes were quickly peeled and added, more vodka was brought out, bowls of red and blackcurrants (of which there were plenty) picked for dessert, a home-made cheese brought up from the underground cellar. Home-made black bread and butter and eggs were always plentiful. If there were not enough beds to go round, the younger generation would be asked to move in together, mattresses were laid on the floor and a room in this way vacated for a more senior guest. At such moments everyone would lend a hand, but there was never any pressure about this. As teenagers, we would decide among ourselves who would help with what. Newcomers and friends all joined in. We picked fruit, we carried water from the lake to water the flower gardens, we collected the eggs, we got honey from the beehives (Paul and I loved doing this). We went out into the woods to pick bucketfuls of wild strawberries, or mushrooms, we helped with hay-making. But if anyone preferred to sit under a tree and read or sleep, no one disturbed him or pressured him. There was plenty of privacy and freedom to do as one pleased or indulge in light romance.

In the evenings when it began to grow dark some of us would go across to the Stackelberg cottage to sing Russian songs. 'Who wants to sing first or second voice?' Moussia would ask and, coming to an agreement, we launched into what we thought perfect harmony.

It is difficult today to imagine the simple mode of life of those days in that little corner of Europe.

Even as a young girl, I would often disappear with a book under a distant tree or sit in the boat with the oars drawn in, letting it glide on the calm lake. There was only one volume of Dickens on our shelves, *Nicholas Nickleby*. I can still remember weeping bitter tears over it. I wrote to my mother and asked her to bring me other books by Dickens, and gradually by the time I was fourteen I had a library of my own of most of his works. I still have my copy of *David Copperfield*, inscribed to me on my birthday in 1929.

At about that time a tutor, Vaska Abels, was hired for the summers, largely to work with my cousin Goga who needed coaching. But he also spent time with me directing my Russian reading. Since we now attended a German-speaking school, our Russian studies were rather neglected. He introduced me to Pushkin, Lermontov and Aksakov, and we spent many an afternoon reading aloud and talking about poetry. I remember so well the thrill when I first read *War and Peace*. Pierre was, of course, my hero. Abels was a clever and charming young man, who later became a brilliant lawyer in Germany. He came to us several years running and became a friend of all of us, children and grown-ups. Inspired by Abels, I also began to read more German poetry; my favourites were Rilke and Heine. Sometimes I would escape somewhere to the back of the house – there was always enough space to lose oneself if one felt like it – to copy out large chunks of poetry into a thick copybook with a hard black cover. I kept this book for many years and jotted down all sorts of personal notes in it; but it disappeared with so many cherished things that we left behind in Kallijärv . None of us could have predicted that unforeseen circumstances would take each one of us far away, and that the rest of our lives would be lived far from the home where we grew up.

Every season had its memorable moments. In autumn new smells reached you, the smells of hay and of mushrooms. Mushrooming and hay-making were activities in which everyone joined, children, grown-ups, maids, and in later years visitors from many parts of the world. It was also the time for picking hazelnuts and there were lots of them. We would round up everyone we could and set out with large baskets which contained a delicious picnic, and would later come back along the 'big path' to the gully. There we would stop at the outskirts of the forest and plunge into the thicket of nut-trees. Pushing back the branches, we wound our way through the trees, chatting and calling to one another or singing 'round' songs in order not to lose each other. After filling our baskets, we sat in the sun to peel off the outer skins, lifting the young nuts, still pale green in colour, out of their shells looking like polished pebbles.

From an early age I remember the days of the first snowfall. We would wake up to find that everything was white. Dashing to the window in bare feet, we would look out on a landscape which had changed overnight. Then for the first time our thoughts would be directed towards Christmas.

After Uncle Sasha and his wife Zoria came to live with us we always had a huge Christmas tree. The tree was brought in to the house secretly when we were meant to be asleep. But more often than not we would be peeping through the keyhole or a chink in the door. 'They've brought it, they've brought it … !' one of us nearest to the keyhole would announce. Back in bed we speculated what our presents would be. The drawing-room now remained locked until the next evening, the final wonderful moment when the huge gong was sounded to call us in. It was to our Uncle Sasha that we owed such delightful secrecy, and not only this, for he understood that a child wants its celebrations separately, and so he gave us the beauty of the

decorated tree to wonder at first, and then a second transform-
ation when, one by one, he lit the wax candles which he had so
carefully arranged on the tree, as we stood speechless in front
of its glittering splendour. Then we all sang 'Stille Nacht' or
some other carol, before the opening of our presents could
begin, and the gifts we children had been making in secrecy for
the grown-ups were presented. Moura would arrive on Christmas Eve, adding to the excitement. But at that time of year she
only stayed for a few days. On the twelfth night the tree was
dismantled and the decorations were put away for another
year. It was only after this that the real freezing cold winter
began, and sledges and skis were brought out.

It was in summer, especially all through the 1930s, that
Kallijärv came into its own. My brother Paul was home from
Salem; Uncle Sasha had also taken his annual holiday; Baron
and Baroness Bengt Stackelberg came every year and settled in
a tiny house next door which had been converted from a
winter bee-house (beehives had to be kept under cover in the
cold winters) into a two-room cottage. Mitia and Marina,
their two children, were constant summer companions. Other
cousins and schoolfriends often came as well from Tallinn.
There was no money for organised games, but we played
volleyball, and bathing in the lake was a daily ritual. The house
was only about 100 yards from the lake, but because the water
was very deep and had cold springs, we children were not
allowed to bathe without the supervision of a grown-up. Some
years previously a young man from the estate had in fact
drowned in the lake. Bathers and non-bathers gathered on the
jetty around noon. Very few of the adults actually knew how
to swim. The only one who swam really well was Uncle Sasha,
who had learned in the army. He would hurl his sixteen stone
into the water, landing invariably in a painful belly-flop. When
H.G. Wells visited us in 1934, he too donned his black
bathing-suit and ventured into the lake, much to our delight.

Sometimes there would be an unexpected thunderstorm and
we would continue to swim in the rain. This was great fun.
Then suddenly, as if from nowhere, there would appear an
opalescent rainbow in the sky, which was reflected in the lake.

I believed in Micky's story that a rainbow means no more rain. Thrilled at the sight of it, we would sing Micky's more colourful version of the English rhyme which she had taught us: 'Rain, rain, go to Spain, and never come back again'. But the rainbow vanished as quickly as it had appeared.

Kira and I loved to sit under the trees in the meadow by the lake and read, taking it in turn to watch over the grazing geese. The weather, as I remember it, was mostly fine. Day after day there was unbroken sunshine throughout June, July and August. It was an idyllic, carefree life for children, and we loved it. We were hardly ever indoors except for meals, when we were never less than twelve. They were blissful and happy months and we looked forward to them all year. In the evenings we would walk down to the water and wait, watching the reflection of the sunset. In the peace of dusk everything was silent, and all adolescent problems and anxieties seemed to drop into the beloved lake.

August was also the time of year of Moura's annual longer visit to us. She usually arrived early in the month and stayed for about three or four weeks. The one and only cart-horse on the farm was harnessed to a rather rickety trap and we would set out to meet her. Our railway station was three miles away and consisted of a hut manned by two station-masters and no porters. As she was usually the only person to get out of the train, they saluted her and helped her on to the platform. There she was, elegant and glamorous, laden with luggage and parcels which we knew contained presents for all of us. We stood there, full of admiration for her clothes, and for her air of familiarity with foreign travel. We regarded her as an omniscient envoy from the great outside world.

The annual preparatory ritual for these occasions was to work us all up to a peak of excitement. It was no doubt Micky's way of trying to build up Moura in the eyes of her children. But we enjoyed the detailed preparations for her arrival. Moura's little room was vacated and thoroughly cleaned by Leeni. A basin, water jug and a portable bidet were brought out of the walk-in cupboard where some of Moura's, and later our, belongings were stored during her absence.

Micky, who was in charge of the keys to this and to various trunks which were kept in the *kamorka*, as we used to call it, had inevitably lost them, and she and I would search feverishly in all the drawers till we found them. We then went into the woods and picked flowers for the veranda and for Moura's room, then we clipped the lilac bushes which surrounded a wooden bench and garden table outside the house, where Moura used to like to sit with visitors in the shade.

When we arrived at the house on our return from the station, Moura would throw open her suitcases and we would stand around while she showered presents on everyone – nothing very extravagant, but in those days and to us they were fabulous. There was always a blouse and bottle of 'Jicky' scent for Micky; a suit, a slip, a book, silk stockings, I can even remember a small manual gramophone, coloured pencils, a postcard album, etcetera, for us; and there was something for everyone. This ritual over, we would all sit down to an early breakfast, Moura automatically taking Aunt Zoria's place at the head of the table, with Micky at the opposite end in her usual place by the samovar. During those summer months we were a numerous 'family'. So now we sat, maybe six grown-ups and ten children, all listening to Moura who presided over us all and pontificated on every subject. Expecting to be adored, and treated as the 'oracle from the west', she made the most of the general atmosphere of heroine-worship.

In the summer months throughout the 1930s right up to 1939, guests came from Tallinn, and from London, Paris, Finland and Germany. One summer our Kotchoubey cousins, my Aunt Assia's children, came from Paris to help improve our French, which was not our strongest language. There was a general coming and going of people of all ages, which brought life and gaiety to Kallijärv. In the evenings everyone joined in charades and other parlour games, and the talking and laughing went on late into the night, while quantities of vodka and cherry brandy were drunk. The younger generation indulged in midnight feasts and other nocturnal pranks, during the 'white nights' when the evenings never became night.

Sometimes we would arrange to meet by the lake, and in the

quiet of the night would secretly go crayfishing by torchlight. Crayfish were a great delicacy. One of the farm labourers, Grigoriy Baikov, had taught us how to catch them. The best time to do this was at night. Some of us would jump up and down on the bank, and the crayfish would slowly back out from under the bank into the lake. One of us would dazzle him with a torch, while another would have his hand in the water ready to receive the emerging crayfish and lift him out of the water. The way to cook them was to throw them live into boiling water. They turned red instantly and were then ready to eat. They were at their best in August.

'Seeing people off' to the station was a regular and important event. We always accompanied friends right to the station; not just one of us, but three or four or more of us would either walk our guests and see them off, or, for older guests, a farm horse was harnessed to a rather rickety cart, which – apart from two driving seats in front – had two long benches facing each other. Everyone would pile in after an argument about who would occupy the driving seat and hold the reins, although the horse knew the way blindfold and hardly required a driver. It would never have occurred to us to leave the 'seeing off' to a farmhand. Guests had to be taken care of properly right to the train.

A popular pastime in which everybody joined was volleyball. It was always played after dinner, and even Moura sometimes participated but more often sat with the other older onlookers watching the game, which we played in a state of great excitement and amidst much good-natured noise and shouting. Although to an outsider these games may have looked unruly, I must have learned something because I later became captain of my school volleyball team.

We were a great family for celebrations. There were plenty of occasions to celebrate: birthdays, name days, someone's last evening, passing of exams. We children would usually instigate these occasions ourselves. They were marked by the packing into baskets of raw potatoes, lashings of butter, kvass, and in later years vodka. Then in the evening we would set out to a favourite spot in the woods where we would make a

17 Tania, aged three,
in St Petersburg

18 Mushrooming at Kallijärv.
Left to right: Kira, Paul
and Tania

19 & 20 Kallijärv in winter

21 *Left:* Tania reading on the lake at Kallijärv

22 & 23 *Below:* Kallijärv in summer

24 *Top:* A family group, 1924. *Left to right:* (*standing*) Kira,
    Moura, Berndt; (*seated*) Micky, Zora with Alexandra,
    Aunt Cossé; (*front*) Paul, Goga and Tania
25 *Centre:* Micky presides over tea
26 *Bottom:* Staff and children. *Left to right:* (*standing*)
    Roosi, Tania, Kira, Paul, Sylvie; (*seated*) Leeni, Goga,
    Alexandra, Micky and Helmi

bonfire and bake the potatoes in the ashes. Somebody would begin a story and the next person had to continue it – Helmut von Schulmann, a great family friend, was particularly good at this. Often after the story-telling we would sing Russian or German songs late into the evening. One of the best celebrations and, for me at least, the most memorable, came in the summer of 1933. Preparations had been made to celebrate Paul's twenty-first birthday. Liuba Hicks, an old friend of my mother's of Petrograd days, had brought Molly Cliff and her son Tony from London to stay at Kallijärv. August was the month when Tony too was to be twenty-one. A dance was planned and thirty or more friends and relations of all ages were invited to celebrate the joint birthdays. A band from the nearest small town had been engaged and Roosi mobilised her friends from the village to help with the preparations. People arrived throughout the day, from Helsinki, from Tallinn and from all over Estonia. Food was laid out on the large balcony table. It was a perfect, hot, clear, starlit evening. We danced on the lawn and even up the hill, wandered about into the wood, swam in the lake by moonlight. Even Micky stayed up to all hours, if only to keep a beady eye on the younger members of the party. Everyone who was present that night cherished its memory.

Unfortunately, even at Kallijärv the summers had to end and we children had to resume our studies. When I was about eleven it had been decided that we older children should attend a school and no longer be taught by aunts and tutors at home. Enquiries were made and it was decided that the coeducational high school for the German-speaking minority in Wesenberg, a town in the centre of Estonia, was the most suitable for us. It had an excellent reputation, largely due to its outstanding headmaster, Dr von Berg. My Aunt Zoria and Uncle Sasha, who were in charge of us, had rented a small, ugly house in the town. Aunt Zoria, her two small daughters, Alex and Nathalie, their nanny, Goga her stepson, who had now come to live with us, my cousin Kira, my brother Paul and I, as well as Micky, all spent the school terms in Wesenberg. Uncle Sasha had taken a job in Narva with the Estonian Shell Co. and was able to join the family only at weekends. I don't think that Aunt Zoria liked the arrangement very much, because after a year or so she decided to give up the house in Wesenberg and to take her young family back to Kallijärv. Micky and I moved to the house of yet another 'aunt', Baroness Lotte Dellings-hausen, from where I continued to attend school. But a month at Christmas and at Easter, and three months during the wonderfully long summer vacations, were always spent in Kallijärv.

Our school at Wesenberg was one of the German-speaking minority schools. The oldest of these was the Domschule (Cathedral School) in Reval (now Tallinn), founded in the fourteenth century. After the end of Catholic supremacy in Reval in 1561, boys were trained there for the Lutheran clergy. Later it became the preparatory school for the famous university of Dorpat, and boys from all classes, but largely from the Baltic nobility, were prepared there. The *Ritterschaft* had been responsible for its finances. With the establishment of Estonian independence, the cultural freedom of the minority schools was guaranteed. As a consequence the government was well-disposed to German-speaking schools, which continued to maintain their high standards.

The pupils came from Baltic landowning families and from the Baltic professional classes, and the élitist atmosphere made us rather snobbish. Since our school was coeducational, we were used to an easy relationship between boys and girls at an early age. In any school it is true that the quality of teaching depends on the individual teachers, and ours, on the whole, were cultivated, interesting people. We were treated very much as equals and were well prepared for the final *Abitur* exam which we took when we were seventeen. We were encouraged to read widely and I think received a good general education. Dr von Berg, the headmaster, encouraged discussion of books and of current affairs, and instilled in us an independence of mind and a feeling for literature. His speciality was German literature. An enthusiast himself, he passed on to us his enthusiasm. Goethe was his passion and he analysed and read with us *Faust* and *Italian Journey*, which he loved. He read our essays with great care and discussed very seriously any ideas we may have produced. His lessons tended to be more like university lectures. In his school bad marks were our only punishment. With Aunt Cossé we had come to accept the idea of punishment as the sanction for poor performance or bad behaviour, but now we were faced with a new state of affairs in which such action played no part. A polite and understanding smile was all we got if our work did not come up to scratch. At first we were completely nonplussed. We were not quite ready at that early age to be treated as adults with a full sense of responsibility for our own actions and behaviour. As with many other aspects of life in Baltic society, a sense of 'honour' was enormously strong and was a guiding principle of conduct in the school. Although seldom actually stated, we were aware of the very high expectations for us held by the staff.

After the exodus of the Balts to the part of Poland occupied by the Germans in 1939, Dr von Berg opened a school near Posen for the children of Baltic families which was also attended by some ethnic German children. He refused to compromise and bravely stood up to Nazi ideas with great courage.

Several things stand out in my memory of my days at school. I remember our physics master very clearly. He was tall and had a deep, commanding, sensuous voice that we girls found irresistible. He was the only member of staff of Estonian origin, but he was not on the full-time staff and only came twice a week to the school. I think he may have felt a little isolated which explains why he was so aloof; but that only added to his attraction for us. I remember my English lessons where, thanks to Micky, I spoke better English than our uninspired and old-fashioned teacher, Fräulein Czerny, and so had little to do except help her correct my classmates' books. I remember our excellent history teacher, Fräulein von Mickwitz, who greatly admired Voltaire and his influence on Frederick the Great, giving us a lively picture of his philosophy of life. I remember singing the St Matthew Passion in St Nicholas's Cathedral in Tallinn, for which the Lutheran pastor had trained the choir; and the memorable occasion of my first concert, when we were taken to hear the Danish violinist Cecilia Hansen who had come to play in Tallinn.

On the whole we enjoyed school and worked hard. In classes of not more than twelve it was possible for the teachers to give us individual attention, to which we were usually ready to respond.

I had two great friends, Gisela von Harpe and Tania Novitskaya, and we three spent a great deal of time together. Tania's parents were pure Russian. There was a great bond between us: our first language was Russian and we were members of the Russian Orthodox Church, while for the majority of the school German was the first language and they belonged to the Lutheran faith. We were both very proud of being 'different'.

Helmuth Russow and Ricko Neff were among my school-friends who often came to Kallijärv in the holidays. Ricko Neff was a gifted and independent-minded person who was always stimulating company. He had inherited from his father, who had been killed in the 1914 war, the remnant of a beautiful estate south-east of Tallinn to which he was deeply attached. We were close friends and had similar views on many things, including political matters, particularly in relation to the emerging National Socialism in Germany and its effect on the Baltic States. However, our relationship never led even to an embrace, though for many years he wrote me what were almost love letters until the war broke off our correspondence. He was one of the few people who refused to leave on the German ship which took the Baltic population from Estonia to German-occupied Poland in October 1939. He did not believe the Nazi propaganda and decided to stay on and see how things would develop. It was a brave decision. It was all the more tragic when a few weeks later he was stabbed to death by a local man in a fit of petty jealousy.

Although in 1932 the Nazis had not yet taken over the government of Germany, they had begun to appear as a threat to peace and their influence was inevitably infiltrating the vulnerable Baltic States. Among the friends I made at school and at Finn, the finishing school where I spent six months after leaving Wesenberg, divisions became sharper concerning attitudes taken towards Hitler and National Socialism. We were divided into two camps and feeling ran high on both sides. The middle-class families were, strangely enough, those to whom National Socialism appealed most, because they felt that their own importance in Estonia would be promoted by a Nazi victory in Germany. Some members of the Baltic aristocracy had listened readily to Nazi propaganda, others believed that National Socialism would effectively oppose and bring about the downfall of Communism. Some, on the other hand, distrusted the Nazi movement and felt that the success of the Nazis in Germany would inevitably lead to a European war which would involve Russia, and threaten the survival of the independent Baltic States. They had no desire to become the subjects of the Third Reich on those terms. But none of the Balts anticipated what in fact turned out to be their fate – a forced exodus from their homes, a temporary settlement in German-occupied Poland, followed by flight before the advancing Russian armies.

As well as the arguments and discussions I had with school-friends and others, my awareness of the political forces at work in Estonia was sharpened through my long-standing friendship with Helmut von Schulmann, who was a frequent summer visitor to Kallijärv, and who used sometimes to come over from Tallinn in the winter as well. I had known Mut, as we called him, from a very early age and regarded him as a close friend. But he became even more important in my life when I began to want information about people and issues which were beginning to affect me. I suppose he was nearly forty when he first came to Kallijärv. It must have been partly because we were otherwise surrounded mostly by women that he had a great influence on us and played such an important part in our lives. True, there was Uncle Sasha, but he was not there all the time and was a dear, kind uncle whom we loved, rather than an intellectual whom we admired. I cannot remember a time when I didn't know Mut. He was always full of fun. A highly intelligent and cultured man and, as a journalist, in touch with world affairs, he was not only well-informed but also open-minded. He was less hidebound than most people and had less of the narrow snobbery which affected many of the Baltic nobility.

For ten years between the two world wars he had a column on the German-language daily newspaper *Revaler Bote*. He wrote amusing and witty articles with an undertone of great knowledge and seriousness, on every topic under the sun. He was too civilised and had a too highly developed sense of humour ever to be influenced by either Communist or Nazi propaganda. Although he respected some of the traditional Baltic codes of behaviour, he liked to entertain his readers and laughed at some of their shibboleths. He felt that the sense of responsibility on which the Balts prided themselves should be directed towards helping the Estonians to organise their new republic. He argued that since the Balts had lost their allegiance and service to the state (that is, to Imperial Russia), responsibility to one's community and to oneself was ultimately the most important. He was as anti-Communist as most of the Balts in Estonia, but he realised that the Communist régime in Russia was there to stay. Since the Estonians allowed a certain cultural autonomy to the German as well as the Russian and Swedish minorities in their country, he believed that the Balts should adopt an attitude of co-operation towards the Estonians, rather than attempt to insist on the privileges of birth.

With children he was marvellous. He would take infinite trouble over us and had the power to arouse and hold our interest. We always looked forward to his visits. He was happily married, I believe, and had one son called Henrik, but to Kallijärv he always came alone and stayed for two to three days at a time. As very young children we already felt that he really came to see us and not the grown-ups. He spent many hours with us, either building stone houses for his imaginary characters in the woods, or telling us stories which he illustrated most humorously. For me, anyway, he brought the enchantment of fairyland into my life. There was one story which he invented for us in instalments. We had built a little house which we called 'Kungle Bink', and at every visit we would disappear to our enchanted secret place in the wood to wait anxiously for a further episode about the little people living in 'Kungle Bink'. Our secret place was near a tiny stream where we would watch the movements of tadpoles in slimy frogspawn. We used the damp dirt from around it to act as cement to build the house for our imaginary wood people. Occasionally we would walk further into the forest where we would watch men cutting turf. The forest was full of surprises. Sometimes an elk would suddenly appear and on seeing us disappear into the thicket.

As I became older I was increasingly aware that the Russian influence on me was much stronger than any other, and although I lived in Estonia surrounded by Balts, I knew little of their history and their early relations with the local population. Kallijärv was a society ruled by Russian women, and Uncle Sasha, who might have told us about the Balts, was more interested in things Russian. It was Mut who told us about our Baltic background and about the time when the Baltic population first came to our part of the world, and how a body of the Order of the Teutonic Knights set out in the fourteenth century to conquer and bring Christianity to this then pagan area.

We loved to hear his many stories, sometimes invented as he went along, but he also had a great repertoire of ancient folk tales. There is one he told us which I made him repeat over and over again. It was the story of 'Taras Bulba', the famous Cossack chieftain who crept back into the Polish stronghold where his son Ossip was being tortured to death on the square. In his agony the boy called out, 'Father, can you hear me?' Out of the crowd came the reply, 'I hear you.' It has always remained with me that if you cannot help you must at least bear witness.

Whenever he came to Kallijärv Mut was always ready to stimulate a discussion about any subject or problem which we cared to raise. He fostered my political and historical awareness, even if I didn't always agree with his views, at a period in my life when it was impossile not to feel passionately engaged in the increasingly serious struggle between Nazi Fascism and its opponents.

From the time he was fourteen, my brother Paul and I began to live rather separate lives, apart from the holidays which were always spent at Kallijärv. Paul had been sent away to Kurt Hahn's school at Salem in Bavaria; and when he was eighteen he was called up for compulsory military service, to which all Estonian subjects were liable. He had a very rough time: conditions in barracks were appalling in those days and he became seriously ill. He was diagnosed as having typhoid and for over a week lay close to death. We were desperately worried, the more so because we were not allowed to see him. He was taken to the military hospital in Narva and only Uncle Sasha and Pastor Egon Pallon, the Lutheran pastor who had confirmed Paul and who was a close family friend, were allowed to visit him, and gave him great support. When the crisis was past, but Paul was still very ill, I begged Uncle Sasha to take me to see him. I shall never forget the hospital, the first I had ever visited, full of very sick people, and my first sight of Paul, who looked more ill than I had thought possible. He was so weak that he could hardly speak, but we sat with him for a while. I managed not to cry in front of him, but when I left the hospital I could no longer control myself and sobbed and sobbed on Uncle Sasha's shoulder at the realisation of what Paul had been through. But he recovered and was given several weeks' sick leave, which he spent at Kallijärv and which he claimed almost made up for the illness.

Among the many guests who visited in the course of those marvellous summers in the 1930s was H.G. Wells, who came to stay on his way back from a visit to the USSR in 1934. He was then an energetic sixty-six. My mother was clearly nervous about whether he would find Kallijärv too primitive and uncomfortable, but he was charming to everyone and fitted in very well, and even joined in hay-making with us all. But he rather embarrassed me one day by asking me to persuade Moura to let him pay for improvements and for bringing electricity to Kallijärv. We all thought Kallijärv wonderful as it was, and the idea of 'improving' it horrified us.

One day he suggested that I come for a walk with him. 'Do you think Moura was Gorky's mistress?' he said in his high-pitched voice. 'She tells me she was his secretary. Well, *I* have a secretary and she is not my mistress.' I said that I hadn't really thought about it and, strange as it may seem, it was true. I was so 'innocent' and childlike, even at eighteen, that such things had not worried me. I was later to find out more about the reason for this question.

At Kallijärv H.G. worked all morning and joined us at the lake before lunch. He was at the time putting the finishing touches to the second volume of his autobiography, the last chapter of which ends with the words: 'I am finishing this autobiography in a friendly and restful house beside a little lake in Estonia.' I read *Mr Polly* and *Ann Veronica*, and when I came to England for the first time a few months later he gave me an inscribed copy of his *Outline of History* 'to understand history as it should be understood'. We became good friends and after I was married during the war he often came with Moura, or on his own, to stay for a few days at a time, with me and my baby son in the peace of the Oxfordshire countryside. But all through the war he never stayed away from London for long. He was still writing, but he was both angry and disillusioned with the indifference of the world to his prophetic novels and warnings of disaster.

Kallijärv continued to exercise its charm on the many people who came to visit us. One English friend who visited in 1938 wrote to me on his return to London:

> Kallijärv quite unsettled me and made me doubt the excellency of English civilisation. It seems to me that you have a much better way of living (this does not refer to the vodka). Here there is no room to breathe: we are over-impressed by simple sums of addition – the longer the numbers, the greater the speed, the more progressive we think ourselves. I could become quite lyrical about Estonia – in fact am.

These words were a spontaneous reaction to the freedom of spirit which he had found in Kallijärv, but they took little account of the realities of the Estonian political situation, threatened as it increasingly was by both Nazi Germany and Russia.

Almost the last guest from England before the outbreak of the Second World War was Bernard Alexander, who followed me from London to Kallijärv by air. I had recently met him in London through a mutual friend. He had just been called to the Bar and told me that he was planning a visit that summer to Soviet Russia and wanted to improve his knowledge of Russian beforehand. As I was going to be on holiday in Estonia at the time, I suggested that he visit us in Kallijärv on his way to Russia. I thought no more about it, but as the semi-cargo boat on which I had sailed from Tilbury docked in Stettin, there in the evening light was Bernard waiting on the quayside. We spent a few hours together until it was time for the boat to continue the journey to Stockholm. There, when we reached Stockholm, he was again waiting on the quayside, having taken an aeroplane so as to be there before we docked for the night. The next day he flew on to Tallinn to await the arrival of my boat in Estonia, and was quite ready to accompany me to Kallijärv. 'My family will be surprised and suspicious if I arrive with an unannounced escort from London about whom they know nothing' I told him. 'You had better spend a day or two sightseeing in Tallinn and I will prepare them at home for your arrival.'

When he did eventually arrive he told me later that he was a little surprised, because he claims that he was never introduced to anybody and he never discovered who was who in our numerous household; that as he tried to open the door into the bedroom which had been indicated as his at the end of a dark corridor, it fell in on to the floor, as it was – so he says – unsupported by anything so prosaic as hinges. His bed, he told me, was harder than he had been used to even when he was at boarding school, and at meals everyone talked at the same time in Russian, German and English without bothering to talk to him in any of the languages. Despite these hardships, Bernard seemed to enjoy what was nevertheless another wonderful summer. He got on famously with Aunt Zoria and with everyone else.

'He is intelligent, I admit,' said my mother, 'but he is not for you. He has a cold analytical lawyer's mind and a temperament too different from yours.' But in the end Moura's remarks had the opposite effect to what she intended. At first I didn't even like him. We saw things in a very different light. We had an entirely separate circle of friends in London. We disagreed about politics, about religion and, as I soon realised, about almost every subject. He made me angry, he reduced me to tears. But he was different, and this intrigued me. He minded inaccuracies of thought and generalisations (especially about political issues). His point of view was new for me but it was, I felt, sincere. My friends warned me that it could not be possible to invent two people more unalike. But when we met again in London the ball had started rolling; I too fell in love.

CHAPTER X
Aunt Zoria

Kallijärv and my schooling were both of great importance in shaping my life, but it was at Wesenberg that I became really aware of another very strong influence and one that I was not fully to understand for some time.

Aunt Zoria was short and very slim, a St Petersburg Russian, highly intelligent, unemotional, an intellectual, unlike most of our Baltic relations, but also dry, cynical, occasionally kittenish and very self-sufficient. She was not an easy person because she was uncompromising in her likes and dislikes. She influenced us in a number of ways, and for many years her opinion carried great weight with me.

Her father's estate, Onstèpol, was near Yamburg, not far from the border between Russia and Estonia. Like so many of her class, her family had a residence in St Petersburg. Zoria spent the winters there, where she was a lady-in-waiting to the Tsarina at all special functions. Her father, who had been Chief of the Russian General Staff, had died when she was a young girl. Both her brothers, to whom she had been very close, were killed in the First World War. Zoria's family was very much English-orientated, and two of her cousins had been sent to England to study at Cambridge University. In 1920 Zoria's fiancé was wounded and died while in command of a regiment of the Yudenich White Army in which my Uncle Sasha was also an officer. When this news reached Aunt Zoria, civil war was raging in Russia, and she decided to leave Russia and cross into Estonia, which by now was independent. Frontier lines were still uncertain. Riding on horseback, together with some of the men from their estate, and driving a herd of cows before them, they crossed into Estonia. She had great courage and determination.

Uncle Sasha was someone who needed to be loved and cared

for. He was my father's youngest brother and our guardian after our father's death. As a young man, he had been a professional cavalry officer in Tsarist Russia and had fought with the Second Russian Army in the 1914-17 war, receiving a decoration for bravery. He was not as imaginative or well read as Zoria. He saw things in black and white. After the fall of the Tsar and the October Revolution he had fought with the White North-Western Army against the Bolsheviks. His allegiance to the Tsar and everything the monarchy stood for was absolute and uncritical. The Bolsheviks were anathema to him, and all his life he hoped to have a crack at them and help restore the monarchy. He combined the qualities of a first-class soldier with such aristocratic virtues as courage, honour and *noblesse oblige*. He was hot-tempered and often irrational; he could also be extremely maudlin. As a young officer he had enjoyed his privileged life with all its trappings. Memories of the past always remained strong with him and he, like many other members of the aristocracy, was not really fitted to face the realities of life. He loved Russia and the Russian people, despised the Germans, though not the Balts, and married three times, women of pure Russian descent. To all of us he was a kind of cosy paterfamilias whom we dearly loved. He had married young and had a son, Goga, by his first wife. But when his best friend was wounded in battle and, dying, had begged him to take care of his fiancée, Zoria, Uncle Sasha was so moved that he took this request quite literally. He was already at that time divorced from his first wife and now proposed marriage to Zoria. He was a true romantic. But they were in every way totally incompatible. Never had there been a less suitable marriage.

When she first came to Kallijärv we found her rather unapproachable, and there were times when, as a child, I positively hated her. On occasions she could be sarcastic and silently disapproving, both of which characteristics are disconcerting and puzzling to children. For example, when Moura, towards the end of a visit to us, would be making preparations to return to Sorrento or to Berlin, Micky, as always on these occasions, would begin to fuss around and become strained due to her own sadness at the impending departure. My brother and I too were sad at the thought of separating again. It was the custom in Russian households when bags were already packed, just before a departure, for everybody in the house to be called together to sit on any available chair for a moment of silence to bless the traveller on his way. This ritual, before Moura's departure, two or three times a year, was usually performed around midnight. The late hour and the sad atmosphere of parting contributed to my distress on such occasions. I can't remember if Paul and Kira wept, but I certainly did. The moment of silence over, Aunt Zoria would jump up, look around disapprovingly and retire to her room. 'She thinks I am a baby to cry,' I used to think, and I hated her for this.

Many, many years later Aunt Zoria told me that she was not disapproving of me, but what used to make her indignant were the late-night departures staged by Moura to play on our emotions, and the effect these always had on us children. In theatrical terms Moura was the star. She had to be the centre of attraction. We all learned this with the years, and sometimes we resented it. But as small children we didn't question her right to behave in this self-centred way; on the contrary, we rather admired it. However, we were somewhat relieved when life returned to everyday normality and we were no longer expected to respond to the constant emotional demands she made of us.

My cousin Goga came to live with us when he was about ten. His mother had remarried and he was now to be brought up by our uncle and Zoria, with their two little girls Alex and Nathalie, his half-sisters. He was my age almost to the day, and lived with us until the age of seventeen. When we moved to Wesenberg with Aunt Zoria and Uncle Sasha he came with us and we attended the same school. Aunt Zoria, it always seemed to me then, was very hard on him. He was a strange and unusual boy, who irritated her, and although she did her duty by him she showed him little affection. He had a very vivid imagination and used to half-invent, half-claim as true the most improbable stories. The only one of us who would listen patiently to him was my brother Paul, who was quiet and retiring as a boy, and with whom Goga shared a bedroom. From an early age he was more interested than we were in religion. He was not, however, cut out for schoolwork. At one time we used to receive weekly reports at school and his were always bad. The result was that in the end, because bad marks were expected of him, he lost interest in trying to do better. Aunt Zoria would make sarcastic remarks to him and compare his marks to Paul's and mine. But instead of leaving it at that, the moment my Uncle Sasha set foot in the house on a Friday she would call him into her room. A few moments later he would emerge as the irate father and call for Goga, accusing him of laziness and ingratitude towards his stepmother.

Uncle Sasha loved his son, but he thought that it was the right thing to do to be tough with a boy. Yet strangely enough, as a child I blamed Aunt Zoria for whipping up this anger in my uncle. Perhaps it was because I felt that she could have stopped him, and because I realised that he was not a very rational being, whereas she was a thinking person. I felt that he was behaving in this way because he thought it was expected of him. How I dreaded those Fridays. Even today I see the scene in my dreams. Too frightened myself at the time to say anything at home, I wrote a carefully camouflaged essay on the subject at school which won me a prize, probably because I felt so strongly about it.

In the freedom of country life children are less exposed to tensions between grown-ups. Now, in the cramped surroundings of the town house in Wesenberg, I became aware of the tension between my uncle and aunt. Clearly they were unhappy together, and even as small children we could sense this. In her frustration Zoria was somehow getting at him through Goga. Poor Goga, he too was unhappy, and in a strange way he seemed predestined to be the victim of some tragedy. In the summer of his and my seventeenth birthday he was on a short visit to his mother on the island of Dagö. He had been coming ashore after bathing in the sea during a storm. Just as he was holding on to a metal railing with wet hands it was struck by lightning. The current went straight through him. We were shattered when the news reached us. His body was brought to Kallijärv to be buried in the Benckendorff family vault six miles away. As there was no Orthodox church choir nearby, Baroness Moussia Stackelberg undertook to organise the funeral ceremony. She was a deeply religious and very musical person and so were her two children. Under her direction the four of us practised all day in order to be able to sing the Russian Orthodox requiem mass at Goga's funeral, when the Orthodox priest would come from Wesenberg to officiate. The music is beautiful and very moving. I sang the alto voice and I still remember the solemnity of those days, as we learned our parts and practised for many hours in Moussia's little house, with a lump in our throats and hardly able to believe that the tragedy had really happened. At the funeral we all four sang the stirring music with deep feeling before a large gathering of relatives and friends. But we sang especially for Uncle Sasha and prayed that our voices would help him in his terrible grief.

We did not even see Aunt Zoria during those few days. Immediately after hearing of the accident she had shut herself in her room and did not venture from it. I remember thinking that she had isolated herself to ask forgiveness. But when she emerged from her seclusion she showed no sign of emotion. She never did. She was a very staunch and unrelentingly strong personality. Life had treated her harshly, but as a child one makes no allowances and passes judgment hastily.

For as long as I can remember, a large oil painting of a handsome young officer, whom we knew to have been Zoria's one-time fiancé, dominated her bedroom in Kallijärv. One day when I was already older, and had not only come to terms with my relationship with my aunt but had come to admire greatly her inner strength, we were speaking about the First World War and she told me that both her brothers had been killed in it. I then, taking my courage in both hands, asked her directly about the portrait that hung above her bed. She was as unprepared as I was for this question, and after a moment's thought she got up and opened the chest-of-drawers, and there was the stained uniform which he had worn in battle, lovingly preserved by her throughout the years. She had always appeared so logical and rational, always in control and never showing any feelings, but here she was revealing a passion more intense than I had ever encountered. It was made all the more chilling by her lack of histrionics at that moment. I came then to understand a great deal more about Aunt Zoria. For one thing, this conveyed to me more vividly than any stories I had heard the full horror that war and revolution had caused. I was also suddenly deeply sorry for my aunt, though frightened by the morbid love she was still determined to keep alive. Till then I had thought of her as cold and unfeeling. In fact, as a small child I had had an unwilling respect for her but very little love. It was now and later, as I grew up, that I began to feel a deepening affection for her.

I gradually came to realise how much I owed to Aunt Zoria's integrity, her clear and rational brain, her uncompromising realism, and I had also seen a glimpse of the other side of her life and observed the depth of her resources. While she had accepted her fate with courage she had suppressed all emotion. Unlike so many of her generation, she was able to look back on the years preceding the revolution intelligently and objectively and see the faults as well as the strength of the society that had vanished. She always maintained that Tsarist Russia was on the road to social progress just before the First World War: the zemstvos – local government councils – were encouraging education, she said; the Duma was the beginning of representative government; land reform was taking shape under Stolypin. There was the beginning of a new outlook. But the First World War killed any chance of a normal peaceful political evolution. It was important, she used to say, to note this, because it was clear that the Bolsheviks did not start from scratch in matters of political reform, but they were faced with disastrous social conditions brought about to a very great extent by the First World War.

Her religious faith was a great support to her and made her less bitter than she might have otherwise been. She was of course deeply attached to her two daughters, and her love and delight in them greatly mellowed her with the years. In later times we talked very freely and honestly with each other and I owe her a great deal. It could not have been easy to be in charge of Kallijärv during those difficult years with little money and no adult companionship. It was she who had kept the whole household together.

There was another event which remains vividly in my memory and which again revealed a different Aunt Zoria to me. It impressed on me not only her ability to cope and to tackle a new situation, but also her obvious compassion and steadfastness in doing so. In 1932, a few days before Moura was to return to England after one of her annual visits, the news came through that my great-grandmother on the Zakrevsky side and her daughter aged sixty had at last received permission to leave the Soviet Union and come to live with us in Estonia. For many months we had been living in hope that this permission would be granted, and in anticipation a two-room extension had been built on to the house to accommodate them. When the revolution broke out the old lady was already paralysed, and her maiden daughter had been looking after her in a house in the grounds of the Zakrevsky estate. It had been impossible to move her and, as can so often happen, she escaped the rigours of the revolution and personal harassment and continued to live in reasonable comfort due to the devotion of the peasants who saw to her needs. But now she was paralysed and bedridden and arrived at our little country station on a stretcher. She was in her late eighties and had come to die among her family. I remember the very white face, serene and gentle in spite of her illness, and the expression of delight when she recognised my mother, whom she had not seen for fifteen years. Her renowned charm and sweetness of character were immediately apparent. Her daughter was very different. She too was already old; her life had been without joy; she was the unmarried daughter who lived at home. Already as a young girl, out of sheer boredom, she had become addicted to opium without which she could not exist.

I was glad that it was not yet time to go back to school and that I was there to be with the old lady during the few weeks which she still had to live. Every day Aunt Zoria and I nursed her, changed bedclothes and turned her over in bed. She had terrible bedsores and was in great pain. But she never really complained. In her youth – and one could still see it – she had been very beautiful. She had lived a life devoted to music and was an accomplished violinist, and she felt herself removed from the social world into which she had been born. Alas, she was already too ill to talk about the past. She only smiled, happy to be with us and to have seen Moura and Moura's children again. But without Aunt Zoria's skill, firmness and gentle approach we would not have been able to tackle the care of such an invalid. I learned a great deal about Aunt Zoria from the way she coped. Twice a day our efforts were rewarded by an angelic smile of gratitude. Four weeks later she died. It was the first time I had been present at a death. It seemed peaceful and a release from great pain. After her death her daughter, Great-Aunt Tassia, continued to live with us. She was a sad figure who rarely ventured beyond her room and complained constantly. From then on a routine was established that one or other member of the family paid her a visit in her room every day. I wish now that I had asked her more about the past, although years of dependence on drugs which now had to be continued in small doses had befuddled her mind by the time she came to stay with us. Zoria was never a person to condone weakness easily. She had the ability, through the perfectly turned sentence or aside, to make you feel uncomfortable or at fault. Great-Aunt Tassia must have seemed to Zoria an example of extreme weakness of character, but Zoria refrained from condemning her and in so doing showed the compassionate side of her character. Furthermore, in ensuring that the old lady received the necessary small doses of drugs regularly, she demonstrated a far greater acceptance of human frailty than I had ever thought her capable of.

Zoria continued to live in Kallijärv for the next few years and we saw her there every summer. The last time I saw her in Kallijärv was at the end of August 1939 just before the outbreak of the Second World War. On August 23 , 1939, the Molotov-Ribbentrop Pact had been signed. This agreement took the whole world by surprise and was certainly inspired on both sides by a desire to buy time before they went to war with each other. It was immediately realised in western Europe that the agreement made it possible for Germany to wage war in the west without incurring the risk of a second front in the east. Under the agreement the Baltic States were recognised by Germany as a sphere of influence of the USSR, and the right to establish air and naval bases on Estonian territory was conceded by the Germans.

During the short campaign which Germany started against Poland on September 1st, 1939, and which signalled the outbreak of the Second World War, Estonia remained neutral. She had firm undertakings from Germany and the USSR that her neutrality would be respected. The Estonian Government hoped that both of these countries would see that it was in their interest that the buffer of the Baltic States should be preserved, but this hope was shattered. On September 1st the Estonian Foreign Minister was summoned to Moscow and presented with a draft Pact of Mutual Assistance, which confirmed the right of the USSR to establish military bases on the Estonian entrance to the Gulf of Finland. After several days of negotiation the pact was signed on September 28th. By this pact both parties bound themselves to abstain from interfering in each other's internal affairs. Similar pacts were concluded by the USSR with Lithuania and Latvia. At the same time a secret protocol was published which had been added to the Molotov-Ribbentrop Pact.

According to the protocol the Balts in Estonia, Latvia and Lithuania were to be repatriated to Germany where they would be granted German citizenship if they wished it. In insisting on the inclusion of this provision in the agreement, the Russians were motivated by the fear that the anti-Bolshevik sentiments of the Baltic nobility would play into the hands of the Germans, and they were anxious to have them removed from the Baltic States. At the same time, Nazi agents and German propaganda let it be known that unless the Balts left their homes they would be massacred by incoming Russians and nobody would raise a finger to help them. The repatriation was supposed to be voluntary, but in fact the Balts had no real alternative, although a few decided to stay. (Thirteen thousand out of the 16,000 Balts in Estonia actually left.) The landowning Balts were offered by the Nazi government a free passage to the recently annexed Polish territory, where they were to be compensated with estates ruthlessly confiscated from the Poles. In some cases the Balts arrived on estates where the Polish owners were still in residence. The latter were forcibly deported to other areas by the Nazis, but many died on the way. Aunt Zoria and her family were caught up in this forced exodus of Baltic families, a particularly painful experience for her – being by origin a Russian rather than a Balt – as the few letters we received from her show.

A letter from Aunt Zoria to us in London written from Kallijärv in October 1939 describes the fate of the Balts:

Yesterday Sasha heard the announcement that the Baltic population in Estonia is 'invited' by Hitler's government to leave their country and re-populate the homes and estates in the Polish Corridor from where the Germans have brutally turned out the Poles. In Estonia, all the rights (schools, jobs) of the minorities will cease to exist, everything will be Estonianised and then Sovietised. It is impossible now for us to get an exit visa to any other country – and I am afraid that we are being taken like cattle to the only country which will take us in – worse luck for us – those of us who would rather do anything than have any truck with Nazi Germany – but we have no choice since nobody here is in any doubt that this little country will be incorporated in the Soviet Union. If I was alone I would not hesitate to stay put. But for the sake of Sasha and the children I have no choice, so we leave for a country I have never liked and a régime which is anathema to me. Some wise friends here left for Sweden and Finland some months ago. Now it is no longer possible. There are of course some Balts who have shown that their sympathies lie with Germany and that has made the Soviets doubly suspicious of all the German-speaking minority. The Soviets are therefore only too happy to see the Balts leave the country.

The letter continues:

A commission has now been set up from the *Landverein*. All
owners of the estates are to make a detailed list of everything
they possess. The property on the estates will pass to the
Estonian Government who will negotiate with the German
Government the extent of compensation each owner of an
estate will receive. The commission will pay for the move
into the part of Poland now annexed by Germany, but it is
laid down that the estates here must be left in complete
order. Everyone I have spoken to advises us to join this
scheme even though it is unlikely that Tania and Paul will
ever see anything of such compensation. Very few people
are prepared to run the risk of staying put. The boats leave in
a week, imagine!

On October 10th the London *Times* published extracts
from a letter sent from Tallinn:

Yesterday was a day of panic among the Balts. After 800
years of prosperous life in this part of the world they are
given 48 hours to decide whether they stay and brave the
possibility of Bolshevik rule or, with a couple of handbags,
sail at once in ships already here, for some part of Poland
that Hitler has occupied. It means losing everything
– businesses they have built up, houses they have owned for
generations – and yet they are practically all going ... Fear
of Communism and their experiences in 1918 made them
feel that they had no choice ... Some tried to change their
mind at the last moment, but it was too late.

For a few months after the expulsion of the Balts the
Estonians thought that the Mutual Assistance Pact would
satisfy the Russians, but on June 11th, 1940, the Estonian
Government was presented with an ultimatum by Molotov,
the Soviet Foreign Minister, claiming that by retaining the

alliance with Latvia, and in other respects, they had violated the Mutual Assistance Pact. In consequence of this the Russians demanded the immediate formation of 'a Government able and willing to secure the honest application of the Pact', and provision was made for the reception of additional Soviet troops in Estonia. Similar ultimatums were delivered to Latvia and Lithuania.

After a display of force by the Russian army in Tallinn, 'elections' took place in July in which a newly formed Electoral Committee declared that the only candidates allowed were those presented by the 'Working People's Union'. According to the Electoral Committee, the result was that 84·1 per cent of the electorate voted and there was a 92·8 per cent majority for the Working People's Union. During the election no mention was made of the incorporation of Estonia into the USSR, but when the Assembly met on July 21st in the Parliament Hall the proceedings began with a resolution that Estonia should join the Soviet Union, which was passed unanimously. Similar resolutions were passed on the same day in Latvia and Lithuania. Thus ended the political independence of the three Baltic States. The final act of the drama was played in the session of the supreme Soviet Council in the Kremlin when the Council accepted the request of the Baltic States for admission to the USSR.

A month later we had a short letter from Poland saying that Zoria and the two girls had arrived there safely. After that we had no further news until 1946 when my husband, who was in the British army in Germany, was able to contact Aunt Zoria after she had managed to reach the British Zone. Eventually we were able to secure permits for her and my cousins to come to England. It required a great deal of adjustment on her part. But she was grateful to have escaped the horrors of war and evacuation and to be in England. Sasha had decided to remain behind in Germany and much later Zoria granted him a divorce, so that he could marry his third wife, Zinaida, a Russian from Narva. She made his old age very happy. Zoria's two daughters soon adapted to life in England. But there was still one more tragedy which befell Aunt Zoria and deeply affected all of us. In 1959 her younger daughter Nathalie (Li) married Sydney Carter, the poet and composer. She was always high-spirited and on holiday in Spain later that year was tragically killed when she recklessly attempted to climb rocks in an area where she should never have ventured without a guide.

Alex, Zoria's elder daughter, who had successfully established herself at the BBC Monitoring Service at Caversham, was able to make a home for her mother in London. Together they lived happily in a little house in Chiswick until Zoria died of a heart attack in 1968.

CHAPTER XI
Moura and H.G.Wells

While we were growing up in Estonia, Moura was living first in Sorrento, then in Berlin and finally in London. Apart from her twice-yearly visits to us in Kallijärv, we had little idea of her activities. In fact, it was not until I joined her in London in 1934 that I found out about the changes in her life that had occurred in the ten years since that idyllic summer with her and Gorky in Sorrento.

In 1927 Maxim Gorky began his periodic visits from Sorrento to the Soviet Union. Stalin was by then asking him to return for good. His wife Ekaterina Pavlovna, who was still living in Moscow and whose opinion always carried great weight with him, was also urging him to return. He himself was beginning to feel that he had been away too long from his reading public. Furthermore, his financial situation was becoming difficult. Gosizdat, the government publishing house, had acquired the rights in his works, and funds, though accumulating inside Russia, were no longer easily made available to him outside the country. Moura realised that the decision in favour of his final return to the Soviet Union was inevitable, and she did not try to dissuade him. She herself was beginning to think seriously about her own future without Gorky.

Gorky had given her a power of attorney over the foreign rights of his books and authority to negotiate for their translation. At the time American as well as German publishers were expressing great interest in Gorky's work and especially in his plays. From Berlin Moura was to act as Gorky's literary agent. She began to spend less time in Sorrento and more in Berlin where she had rented a room. With the help of the American journalist, Barrett-Clark, who had met Gorky and who was then living in Berlin, she translated *Fragments of my Diary* into English.

Through Gorky, Moura had had the opportunity to meet many writers and artists of different nationalities, which now gave her an entry into the literary worlds of Berlin, Paris and London. Among them were the writers Romain Rolland, Romain Gary, Stefan Zweig, Thomas Mann and H.G. Wells. For a few years Berlin was a suitable base of operations for Moura; it was not far from Italy – she still spent long periods in Sorrento; and not too far from Estonia where she visited us.

But by 1931 National Socialism was becoming a real threat, and for Moura life in Berlin became increasingly unsettled. Many liberal and Jewish intellectuals were planning to leave Germany, while others had already done so, and these included many friends she had made through her association with Gorky. The clouds of a future, if not imminent, war were gathering. During her stay in Berlin Moura did not have many financial worries, thanks to Gorky, but now she was beginning to make plans for a move to London. She had visited London several times since 1929, and had re-established contact with H.G. Wells and also (on a basis of friendship) with Robert Bruce Lockhart. By the end of 1931 Moura decided that she would settle in England and we children were to finish our schooling in Estonia and join her later. We realised the necessity of earning our own living as soon as possible, and with the confidence of youth were anxious to do so. My cousin Kira, who had grown up with us, and was more of a sister to me than a cousin, was the first to leave Estonia and to come to London where Moura had arranged for her to stay with a friend. Two years later my brother Paul began to study for a diploma at Harper Adams Agricultural College in Shropshire. Being the youngest and still at school in Estonia, I was to follow the next year.

In London Moura had discovered a renewed interest in H.G. Wells. They had first met in Gorky's apartment in Petrograd during his visit to Russia in 1920 when she had acted as his interpreter. Moura's Russian background had always fascinated Wells. His interest in Russia had been first aroused by a visit to St Petersburg and Moscow in January 1914. In his book *Russia in the Shadows*, published in 1920, he says that he had been asked in September of that year by Mr Kamenev of the Russian trade delegation in London to repeat his visit. This had been followed up by an invitation from Maxim Gorky to stay in his apartment in Petrograd and see the Soviet Union for himself.

During his visit in 1920 Wells came face to face with the realities of the Russian situation. 'Our dominant impression,' he wrote in *Russia in the Shadows*, 'of things Russian is an impression of a vast irreparable breakdown.' Although Wells hated Marxism, he was convinced that the Bolsheviks were the only possible nucleus which could be used for a revival in Russia. He believed that the future of Russia as a civilised power depended upon the success of the Bolsheviks in maintaining their position of control. Their failure would mean a relapse of Russia into a 'state of division, petty civil war and political squalor'.* These views were of course in complete contradiction with the more generally accepted view held in England at the time that the future of civilisation depended upon a liquidation of the Bolshevik régime in Russia to prevent its spread throughout Europe.

During the years while Gorky was in Sorrento, Wells had been living part of the time with his wife and part of the time with Odette Keun, for whom he had built a house in the south of France. In 1927 his wife Jane died of cancer, and by 1928 Wells admitted that he was getting tired of Odette, and was beginning to contemplate other possibilities.

In 1929 he met Moura again in Berlin where he was lecturing. They had not seen each other for eight years, but Wells always claimed that he had never forgotten her since his visit to Petrograd in 1920. Wells tells us in his autobiography that after meeting Moura again there was a period of shilly-shallying in their relationship between 1929 and 1932. Wells himself had not yet made the break with Odette and Moura was moving between London, Berlin and Sorrento; in fact, he says that it was the discovery of correspondence between himself and Moura by Odette Keun in 1931, after Moura had

---

* *Russia in the Shadows*

made her decision to establish herself in London to be near him, that brought about the final rupture in his relationship with Odette and his expulsion from the house near Grasse in the south of France.

By the end of 1932 Wells was pressing Moura to make her life with him and marry him. George Bernard Shaw wrote at the time to a friend that Wells wanted 'to take out an insurance against old age and loneliness which was called marriage'. Moura wanted to keep her independence. She was twenty-six years younger than Wells. Wells himself went about complaining, 'She will live with me, dine with me, sleep with me, but she won't marry me!'

In 1933, after several more visits to Russia, Gorky finally gave up his house in Sorrento and left for Moscow with his son and daughter-in-law. In the late spring of that year, Wells arranged to meet Moura at a congress of the international PEN Club at Dubrovnik. From there H.G. and Moura went to Austria for a holiday, but she again managed to escape from Wells on some pretext, and arrived in Istanbul just in time to say farewell to Gorky and his family who were on their way from Naples to Odessa.

Back in London, Moura established herself in a small apartment near the British Museum. Although she was prepared to be Wells's companion and to escort him on trips abroad and at weekend house-parties, she did not want to marry him or to share a home with him. In her autobiography Enid Bagnold tells of when she lent her home, The Elms in Sussex, to H.G. Wells for his 'honeymoon' with Moura Budberg.

'When you are old,' he said, making his discovery a bit late, 'you only look a fool when you fall in love with a *young* woman.' Moura twinkled at me and I forbore to say – 'You might have learnt that before.' He asked us to his wedding party in a Soho restaurant. There was a long table at which we all sat (perhaps 30 people) ... I went up to Moura to congratulate her. She smiled up at me with calm. 'I'm not going to marry him. He only *thinks* I am. I'm not such a fool.

Marjorie [Wells's daughter-in-law] can go on doing the housekeeping.'

Wells had always been jealous of the Russian part of Moura's life and her relationship with Gorky. Therefore she pretended to him that this relationship had been platonic, but he did not entirely believe her. Moura always insisted to Wells that she could never go back to Russia, and in particular she told him that she could not accompany him when he arranged a visit in 1934 to talk with Stalin. Wells believed her when she said that, although her arch-enemy in the Soviet régime, Zinoviev, was now discredited, she was still liable to be arrested if she returned to Russia and sent to a labour camp, or even summarily shot. He therefore took with him to Russia his son George Philip, but he promised to return alone through Estonia and to stay for a fortnight with Moura and her family in Kallijärv.

When he arrived in Russia, Wells was fêted by the Soviet authorities and given a series of parties where he met numerous literary figures, many of whom were friends of Gorky. These had no hesitation in talking to him openly about Moura. In fact they talked of her as somebody with whom they had frequent contact. It soon became clear to Wells from these conversations that Moura had paid regular visits to see Gorky since his return to Russia, and that she had been there very recently. This was a shattering blow to Wells, who suffered pangs of jealousy, hurt pride and disappointment at such deception.

When Wells arrived in Estonia he confronted Moura with the accusation that she had been to Moscow, not only recently but on several other occasions. In the third volume of his autobiography, *H.G. Wells in Love*, he says that Moura never admitted to any truth in his indictment. 'She stuck to it stoutly that she had been to Moscow only this once. I had misunderstood or Andreychin had misunderstood.' She told him that she had been to Moscow only this once because she 'wanted to see Russia again' and that she 'had never been anything to Gorky but a friend'. Wells knew that this was not the truth, but he tried to believe her. Although he realised that he really should break with Moura, it was equally clear to him that this he could not make himself do. I was in Estonia when Wells arrived in Kallijärv from the Soviet Union, and I well remember his mood of anger and suspicion.

In an entry in his autobiography of June 1935 he writes, 'We have gone on together because of an inability to part. She held on tenaciously. But we were no longer the happy confident lovers we had been.' And a little later he continues that after returning to England in 1934 he went to see his friend Christabel Aberconway and told her some of the things that were troubling him, and she 'unfolded a very prevalent feminine theory':

> 'We all cheat,' said Christabel. 'We cheat not because we don't love you, but because you are such unreasonable things that you would not let us live anything you could call a life if we don't ... Stick to her, H.G., and shut your eyes ... I loved to see you together when you came over from Portmeirion last summer.'

But, Wells continues, 'I cared too deeply for Moura to keep things at that superficial level.' Wells comes nearest to understanding Moura, and the truth of the situation in 1934, when he writes in the third volume of his autobiography, 'Plainly her relations to Gorky – even if they were, as she declares, sexless – were of a nature so intimate and sentimental that she could not be with us together in the same place' (that is, in Moscow).

Wells realised then that his dream of a life shared with Moura was an illusion, and he gave up any idea of marriage. However, he continued to want her at his side and was prepared to accept her for what she was and for what she gave him, though he knew that she was not always frank with him.

Moura had now settled in London and into a way of life with Wells. It was at this point that I came to London. It was an upheaval that I was glad to make, for it had been planned for

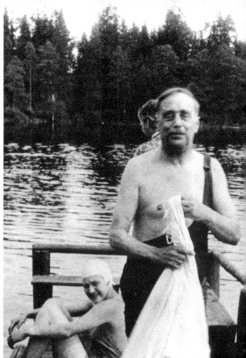

27 *Top left:* Wells sets off rowing, watched by Moura, Molly
Cliff and Tania
28 & 29 *Top right & bottom:* Wells by the lake at Kallijärv

30 & 31 *Above:* Summer 1934 – Tania and Wells
32 *Below:* A family group at Kallijärv. *Left to right:*
Nathalie, Wells, Alexandra, Zoria, Molly, Moura and
Micky

33 *Above:* Moura, Tania and Tony Cliff on a picnic in the woods

34 *Below:* Returning from a picnic. *Left to right*: Princess Zoya Galitzine, Kira, Moura, Paul, Count Constantine Benckendorff and his daughter Nathalie

35 *Top left:* Tania's passport photo – taken before leaving
for England in 1934
36 *Top right:* Reading a manuscript for Secker & Warburg
37 *Bottom left:* Tania with Katharine Ridley on Tania's first
return visit to Leningrad, 1936
38 *Bottom right:* Moura and Tania, 1939

some time that we children would need to leave Estonia if we were to make our way. Kira was by now married, and living in London; Paul had been in England since 1933. Although I was of course very sad to leave Micky behind, I was excited by this new adventure. Many of our friends went to Germany, for there were strong ties between the Balts and the Germans. Our dislike of National Socialism and what we could see happening in Germany ruled that out. Ever since my grandfather Zakrevsky, who had always been a great admirer of England, there had been links with that country, and because of Micky, we all spoke English well; we sensed therefore that it was in England that our futures lay. And so, when Moura wanted me to join her in London, I was delighted to go; it was a move I had been eagerly looking forward to throughout my last year at school.

A room had been found for me in a house in Knightsbridge where Moura and her friend Liuba Hicks were already living. Liuba had married Captain William Hicks, a member of Lockhart's mission, the day before they left Russia in 1918, and so her friendship with Moura went back a very long way. But there was no organised joint existence. We all went our own ways, meeting occasionally, each fending for herself. Moura usually stayed in bed till lunch-time. Much of her morning was spent on the telephone making arrangements with people to drop in for a glass of sherry (which she used to buy in a cask) between 6 and 7.30 p.m., as well as hoping to receive a dinner or lunch invitation. With admirable persistence she would go through a list of people every morning till she had the acceptance of at least several for each day of the week. And if anyone failed to turn up she would telephone to ask why, and insist on another date. She would usually visit H.G. Wells in the afternoons and return to dine with him at his flat or with somebody from his large circle of friends. At weekends Wells was very often entertained in country houses of the rich and Moura always accompanied him. She and I did not see much of each other during the day, but we made a point of looking in on each other on coming home, usually very late at night. But of course Moura was often abroad for long periods, with or without Wells, and nearly always away at weekends: my role at such times seemed to be to invent endless excuses of varying plausibility for friends who – it seemed to me quite unnecessarily – were to be kept guessing as to her whereabouts. I thoroughly enjoyed my freedom, and everything London had to offer.

Liuba Hicks occupied a room above mine. At that time she had a small dress shop of her own. Her husband had died only a few years after they had come out of Russia. He had left no money and Liuba had to fend for herself. She took great care of her appearance and was still very good-looking, with a tiny face and large blue eyes. She had endless energy, largely directed at that time towards trying to persuade one or other of her admirers to marry her. Marriage, however, was not what most of them had in mind. But in the end she did succeed. In 1938 she married Sir Lionel Fletcher, a retired railway engineer who was well off, kind and undemanding. In 1946 they emigrated for tax reasons to Tanzania where they lived until he died.

Moura and Liuba came from different social backgrounds, but the bond between them was their shared experience of the turbulent years of the revolution in Russia. Circumstances had thrown them together then and they remained friends to the end of their days. Both were women of great courage and determination.

Living under the same roof with these two unusual and egocentric ladies was for me an experience which was in sharp contrast to the unsophisticated life of my childhood. I was plunged into their world of unromantic affairs and was the audience of their past, and witness of their present, escapades. I was fascinated but not a little disorientated. I suppose that when at nineteen I first came to live with Moura at close quarters I was too naive and unprepared for her personality. She was not good with young people and, being still a relatively young woman herself, always demanded to be the centre of attention. At her own parties she hardly ever introduced me to her acquaintances and resented it if any of them invited me out. Kira, who had shared an apartment with

Moura in Berlin for a short period, had had the same experience. For an otherwise generous nature she was surprisingly jealous in her personal relations. Her secretiveness about her family affairs was sometimes exaggerated to the point of absurdity. I remember one occasion, soon after I came to live in London, when we arrived at a publisher's dinner given by Jonathan Cape. We were put at separate tables. At my table the place-name, much to my embarrassment, was set for Baron Budberg. It turned out that the invitation had been for him. Moura had never told Jonathan Cape that she was divorced and that Baron Budberg was not in London; nor had she ever told him that she had a daughter. She had disingenuously thought that at such a large gathering nobody would notice if she took me with her, telling me that I had been invited. As a result I was very uncomfortable, feeling myself to be a gate-crasher, and was introduced to nobody. Later, when Jonathan Cape got to know her better and was aware of her foibles, he helped me to see the funny side of the incident and from then on always called me 'The Baron'.

In 1936 Moura again went to visit Gorky in Moscow. Again she did not tell Wells that she was going because she knew how jealous he would be. After she had been in Moscow for nearly a week Gorky fell ill. It was clear that he was dying. Through the intervention of his family she succeeded in prolonging her visa there. But before she left London she had asked me to tell H.G. that she had fallen ill in Paris. She had told him that she was visiting her sister, and was now in a nursing home. I have an entry in my 1936 diary on June 10th:

Pestered by H.G. all week; how is it I don't know the name of the nursing home!? Hate having to tell all these lies. June 11th: dined H.G. (Antony & Flora R.) M. rang from Moscow middle of the night. Told her it would be much better to tell H.G. the truth now ... June 13th: Good. M. has 'phoned H.G. from Moscow telling him she's left the nursing home and flown to Moscow as Gorky was dying and has asked for her. Thank goodness no more lies required. Still have to pretend I knew nothing of all this till today. Fed up being intermediary every time. Makes me look a complete fool... June 18th: Gorky died. M. staying for funeral. Sad.

There is therefore no truth in the legend, started by Moura, that she had been summoned and had responded in a flood of romantic compassion to Gorky's call for her on his death-bed. She promoted this legend largely to placate H.G. Wells. She had in fact gone to Moscow for her annual visit when Gorky became fatally ill, and she managed to extend her visa to be with him. His death was not only a great personal loss to Moura, but it cut her off from Russia for over twenty years. Although there had never been any question of Moura returning to Russia with Maxim Gorky in 1933, she was able to visit him briefly in Moscow once each year till his death in 1936. It is my belief that she missed the stimulation and warmth which had surrounded her in Russia and in Sorrento so much that it changed her whole outlook. Nothing seemed really to matter any longer outside her own personal concerns. Her strength lay in her single-mindedness, coupled with a total lack of scruple, with which she set out to make the world take notice of her. To most of her friends and acquaintances this underlying sadness in her make-up was not apparent. She was not yet recognised and established in London literary circles – as she later became – and all her energy and concentration now went into achieving this.

Moura returned to London immediately after Gorky's funeral, and although she never moved in with H.G. she remained his companion till the end of his life. They had by now come to an understanding of their need for each other, as well as of each other's character. In later years when they both stayed with me from time to time in Oxfordshire, H.G. used to refer good-humouredly to Moura's 'easy way with fact'.

As time went on I began myself to be embarrassed by the different and sometimes conflicting stories she would tell to her friends and acquaintances, and was worried by the demands she would make on me to cover up for her. When I challenged her, I was met with such indignant protestations and such distortions of fact that in the end I gave up interfering. In her eyes anything was justified which helped promote the image she wanted to create of herself. Her charm, which she was able to switch on with telling effect on most people, brought her many admirers. But it was never enough for her. She seemed to be driven by a need – and even a kind of greed – for more admiration. She always had to be the star and to keep her end up required constant scheming and flattery. Some saw through this weakness, but those who were not too deeply involved and enjoyed her company accepted it and were affectionately amused. I remember being angry at the time that her concentration on her own personal affairs seemed to me to be making her indifferent to the vital political issues of Europe in the 1930s. In my youthfulness I did not see that the precariousness of her own personal situation made it impossible for her to adopt idealistic political attitudes on the issues which some of my friends and I felt so strongly about at the time. Moura, above all people, I felt, should concern herself with such matters rather than worry whether A would find out if she had been with B. But she brushed them aside.

The middle and late 1930s when we lived together in London were not then a very happy period for Moura. She had little work of her own. Although we each rented a room in the same house, it was not in any way a home. Sometimes I would join her for dinner at H.G.'s house or at the house of our friend, Molly Cliff, whose kindness and generosity to Moura and me I shall always remember. But more often than not we would meet only late at night or for a moment before going out to dinner. She interfered little in my activities, but occasionally expressed concern about some attachment or other which I might have made and which she thought was unsuitable. But she was always urging me to get married because, I suppose, she felt it would give us security. I liked my bohemian freedom and at the time was anxious to avoid for as long as possible not only security but also marriage. I felt that she was pushing me into a conventional life while she was still determined to maintain her own independent existence free from long-term commitments. But living together in London had gradually changed the roles we adopted and our attitude to each other, and as I grew up I was no longer prepared to be manipulated by her.

CHAPTER XII
London

By the end of my first year in England I was beginning to stand on my own feet. I was making my own friends and was enjoying all the pleasures that London afforded. At first I had had dreams of obtaining some professional qualifications, but I soon realised that we could not afford this, and that it would be necessary for me to find a job as quickly as possible, so that Moura would not have to support me as well as herself in London. On my twentieth birthday H.G. Wells had given me a handsome portable typewriter (which is still in my possession), and after a crash course in shorthand and typing in a small secretarial college I somehow acquired a huge certificate stating that I was a competent shorthand typist. The principal of the college congratulated me on being their first foreign student to have achieved this 'distinction', and sent me for an interview with an organisation called The London Bank in Cannon Street. To my great surprise they said that I could have a job as soon as I could obtain a labour permit from the Under-Secretary of State at the Home Office. Armed with a letter from my new prospective employer, in which it was stated that my knowledge of foreign languages was invaluable to them, and that I was therefore not taking a job from anyone who was British-born, I sat waiting for my turn for some three hours. When finally a policeman called out my name and handed me back my passport with a permit to work for six months rubber-stamped in it, I was overjoyed. My new employers were to pay me three pounds ten shillings a week. My room and breakfast cost two pounds a week. I had thirty shillings to spend. I felt rich.

The ritual of applying for my labour permit to be renewed was to be repeated every three or sometimes six months for the years up to the outbreak of the Second World War. Many people I knew were less lucky than I was and had their applications refused. It was a humiliating exercise and it made me feel for a very long time that the essential characteristic of being a refugee is that however successful one may be, one remains a foreigner in one's own mind. It is difficult not to feel deprived of the same rights to participate, if one has to live in a constant uncertainty as to whether one will be allowed to stay on in the country of residence, or be able to find another employer willing to support an application for a work permit.

My job at the bank turned out to be a ghastly one, and I left after six weeks. The 'bank' was only a façade. In fact it was a 'bucket shop' which advertised shares in a gold-mine called 'Gabey Gold' in Africa – which did not exist. This was later exposed by the *Daily Mail* and my shifty employer was jailed for seven years. I was by then well out of it. I was fortunate enough to find a temporary job with the literary agency A.M. Heath & Co to deal with manuscripts and the foreign correspondence of one of their directors, Cyrus Brooks. Here my surroundings were much more congenial: but there wasn't enough work and Cyrus Brooks himself sent me to Jamie Hamilton with a letter of recommendation, who in turn sent me to see Fredric Warburg. Fred Warburg and Roger Senhouse had just bought out Martin Secker, who had gone bankrupt, having been one of the best and most discerning publishers in the 1920s and 1930s. Fred and Roger both interviewed me and I was given the job. That afternoon I set off to take yet another letter to the Home Office. I still have a copy of it:

To the Under-Secretary of State,
   Home Office   Aliens Department
   Whitehall   January 2nd 1936
Tatiana Benckendorff is to enter into our employment on January 15th in the capacity of secretary and personal assistant (largely dealing with foreign correspondence) and of adviser on foreign books and manuscripts. I shall be grateful if you will extend her permit to work in this country

for the longest possible period as her knowledge of languages is invaluable to us.

F.J. Warburg

The permit was granted and provided a tremendous boost to my self-confidence. It was subsequently renewed every six months without too much difficulty during the five years that I worked for Secker & Warburg.

The staff of the firm was tiny. Apart from Fredric Warburg and Roger Senhouse who had jointly bought the business, there was Martin Secker who had agreed to stay on and help the new directors during the first year, and there was a young clerk, John Pattisson, who had gone into Secker's firm straight from school. His knowledge by now of the technical side of publishing was profound. I shared an office with him and he taught me more than anyone about the publishing business. There was also John Lloyd, who joined the firm as an apprentice. His interest was in typography, book production and design. He was tall, dark and good-looking and only a year older than I was. We were instantly attracted to each other and enjoyed a flirtatious relationship, which only added to the fun and enjoyment of our work.

The great advantage of working in such a small firm was that it was possible to see all the different aspects of publishing at every stage. In those days a book could be produced in six or eight weeks from manuscript to published work. Fred Warburg had a difficult temperament and awkward manner which upset many of his publishing colleagues, but he had a certain integrity which I greatly admired. He made things interesting by involving me and taking me into his confidence, whether we were discussing the contents of a manuscript which he was thinking of publishing, or the problems of the firm, or the idiosyncrasies of his authors. Both at the office and at frequent publishing parties which he and his wife Pamela gave in their apartment, he introduced me to his authors, many of whom became friends. I remember one such evening when, after most of the guests had already gone home, Paul Robeson sang to us his wonderful Negro spirituals, and then for my benefit he switched to Russian gypsy songs, singing in perfect Russian in which I and his wife joined.

Fred Warburg had inherited many fine titles from Martin Secker, but he realised that a new firm needed a definite policy. Motivated by his abhorrence, both as a human being and as a Jew, of Nazism and Fascism, he now set out to publish contemporary political writers. The new Secker & Warburg list was largely radical, anti-Fascist – sometimes anti-Communist – and generally unorthodox. This policy was bound to create serious financial problems for the firm. In the early days it certainly did. But in the long run the company made a great name for itself, and by the early 1940s Secker & Warburg had become one of the most respected publishing houses in London.

Even before coming to England I had witnessed in Estonia the beginnings of Nazi influence, and I was already very conscious of the threat of war from Germany which hung over Europe. It seemed to me that in the end there would be a clash between Russian Communism and German Fascism, and I felt that the former had originally been inspired by humanitarian ideals and that in the end these ideals would triumph over German Fascism. I had visited the USSR in 1936 and knew that it was not the Utopia imagined by some people. The visit had been planned when Gorky was still alive, but despite his death in June of that year – soon after the sudden death of his son, Maxim, which had shattered him – I was able to stay with his family in Moscow. I saw and made friends again with all the members of his household who had been in Sorrento in 1925 and my pleasure at seeing them once more was great. They took so much trouble to show us all the sights, both in Moscow and in Leningrad, and gave us a marvellous time. I had as a travelling companion Katharine Ridley, a distant cousin and close friend. She was the granddaughter of Count Benckendorff, the last Ambassador of Tsarist Russia in England, and was as interested as I was in visiting Russia.

That summer a new 'Constitution' had been published and was being sold in the streets, guaranteeing 'Freedom of speech, freedom of the press and freedom of expression'. I bought a copy and have it still. It was never fully implemented; but people had faith in it, and during our visit Katharine and I (maybe I more than Katharine) were eager to believe that here in the USSR a world of equal opportunity based on trust in the unlimited powers of man was being built. 'The equalitarian beginning of a perfect society,' Walter Duranty had written. We sat and talked and discussed late into the night with artists, painters and university professors every day of our three-week stay in Soviet Russia, and here among the Soviet intelligentsia we were left with the impression of people who had great expectations and faith in a New World. We felt the strong pull of our Russian ancestry and responded readily to the warmheartedness and generosity of the Russian people. Everyone we spoke to seemed to us so enthusiastic, genuine and down-to-earth, and we began to share their optimism. They admitted that there had been a lot of cruelty, but maybe this had been necessary to create a fairer world.

I was never able to share the views and allegiances of those critics of our society who saw salvation only in an extremist political philosophy. But in the mid 1930s I felt like so many liberal-minded young people in England who thought that the only real hope of resistance against Fascism lay in an alliance with Russia, after what they considered to be the failure of the western democracies to stand up to Hitler. Russia was emerging from centuries of ignorance and oppression. The revolution had been necessary because the First World War had destroyed the chance of a peaceful transition to a democratic régime. Because we believed that equality and liberty could be reconciled in Russia, we defended the Communist ideal and refused to believe that Stalin's régime was, in reality, a most brutal form of dictatorship. It was almost impossible for us to credit what we read in the press only a few months after our visit to Russia – that Stalin's 1936 purge had resulted in the death of a great many people, among them some we had met in Russia and trusted. The network of intrigue and the ruthlessness of the power struggle which was going on at all levels of the Party and of the government under Stalin were later revealed to the whole world.

In London I felt drawn to people who were prepared to fight for social justice and were determined to combat Fascism as the greatest threat to peace. I attended left-wing political meetings, went to Fabian lectures and debates, and listened to eminent men, such as Bertrand Russell, C.M. Joad, Harold Laski and others speak.

When the civil war broke out in Spain, without knowing very much about the internal Spanish situation or the background to the war, I believed that it was the first battle in the inevitable war between democracy and Fascism. Several of my friends joined the International Brigade. We felt tremendous excitement at the idea that the future of mankind was in the balance in Spain. The struggle against Fascism was also very much the concern of Warburg's new authors. Among them then were Fenner Brockway, C.L.R. James, Edward Conze, Ethel Mannin, Cedric Dover and George Orwell. Eventually I was also able to persuade H.G. Wells to leave his publisher and become one of our authors. His last three books appeared under the Secker & Warburg imprint.

Many years later Warburg wrote in his autobiography:

Tania ran her affairs, as she ran mine, with spasmodic violence and unusual powers of forgetfulness … She made many mistakes but never a blunder. She understood what none of my colleagues except Senhouse understood: that Secker & Warburg was … not so much a commercial enterprise as a 'movement'. It followed that 'public relations' was the most important of our activities and as a PRO Tania was unexcelled, everybody liked her.

I was twenty-one. I listened, talked, and discussed with enthusiasm things that I did not know enough about. But I learned as I went along, and gradually began to acquire more confidence in my own ability. I had by now made many friends of widely different backgrounds and convictions, which is one of the advantages of living in a large and welcoming city like London. Many of these friendships have lasted for life.

Not all my time was spent worrying about the world. There

were more frivolous, carefree times when I would stroll with friends in the country, or dine at some cheap restaurant, or talk late into the night in someone's flat or house. Or Tony Cliff would invite me to a May Ball in Cambridge, and we would dance all night, and I would get back to London in time to have a bath before going to the office, work all day and repeat the same process in the evening. With Gavin Maxwell I went to the subscription concerts at the Queen's Hall, something we would look forward to all week. There were also late nights at the 400 Club or dinner at the Ivy after having been to a play or to the ballet, and many an evening spent at the Café Royal, one of my favourite haunts. There were delightful weekends in country houses – I remember one country house to which I was quite often invited where weekends were rather formal. Your case was unpacked and your clothes laid out for dinner. I remember my first visit soon after my arrival in London, and coming back into my room, ashamed and horrified to find all my hurriedly packed belongings carefully laid out. On one of these occasions a heated discussion arose which produced a violent reaction from me. 'Nobody takes your left-wing views seriously, darling Tania,' said our host, 'but I love to see your kind heart roused with indignation.' At this I was ready to blow up, but I managed to laugh because I knew that, in spite of his reactionary views, his heart was in the right place.

Secker & Warburg were by now paying me the incredible sum of five pounds a week, and I knew that even that amount was not easily found in a business which was in constant financial trouble. But in those days a good lunch could be bought for five shillings and a snack for very much less. Concert and theatre seats were well under ten shillings. I was usually able to balance my budget, though sometimes I would borrow ten shillings from my landlady on a Thursday and pay it back on Friday. For dinner one relied on being asked out. There was no means of cooking a meal in the house we lived in. But I was frequently invited to delightful dinner parties with friends, or a gallant escort would take me out to a restaurant. Girls in those days very rarely paid for themselves when invited out. And of course there was always the home of my beloved cousin Kira, who was now married to Dr Hugh Clegg and lived in North London. I knew that I could turn to them whenever I wanted to or if ever I was in any trouble. They had been married in the Russian Orthodox Church in London in 1933 before my arrival in England. Hugh had quickly become part of the family to all of us. He had been a practising doctor for many years, but fairly recently had become sub-editor of the *British Medical Journal*, and was soon to become one of the most distinguished editors of that important paper. My income was also supplemented by the occasional translation, on which I would work at weekends and mobilise the help of many of my long-suffering escorts.

I knew that Moura would find money to pay for my summer holidays if I needed it. But more often than not, just before the summer holiday drew near, a cheque would arrive from H.G., and on my twenty-first birthday he also sent me twenty pounds which seemed like a fortune. From this large fund I bought a beautiful long evening dress in Knightsbridge which cost two pounds ten. The balance supplemented my income for weeks to come, and I was even able to lend a pound to one or other of Warburg's more poverty-stricken authors!

In the summer of 1937 Barbara Greene, a cousin of the talented Greene brothers, and I set out in her little Austin 7 for Estonia. Barbara was always game for an adventure and so was I. Two young girls travelling alone in a ramshackle car provided much amusement wherever we stopped on the way to Berlin. Once there, we stayed with Hugh Greene – later Sir Hugh Carleton Greene – who was then *Daily Telegraph* correspondent and had recently been appointed chief correspondent in Berlin. To celebrate his appointment we dined that night on a terrace, and every member of our party kept nervously looking over his shoulder, while talking in whispers and taking advantage of the fact that in the open air it was less dangerous to speak.

Two years later, Hugh Greene, along with five other journalists, was ordered to leave Germany. This action by the German Government was a reprisal for the expulsion from

London of the correspondents of the *Nationale Zeitung*. Hugh Greene had in fact been courageously reporting for some time the truth about Nazi activities in Germany, without in any way mincing his words.

From Berlin we drove through Latvia visiting friends on the way. I remember the enormous relief of being able to talk freely with people after a week of the tense atmosphere we had experienced while travelling through Nazi Germany. When we finally reached Estonia, Barbara was as enchanted by Kallijärv as were all the friends who visited it.

Back in London there were, of course, moments when I began to get restless. Although I enjoyed my work at Secker & Warburg, I was now more qualified and more confident, and I began seriously to think of moving to another publishing house which would give me more scope and also better pay. But the main difficulty for me in those days was still the question of the alien's work permit and the risk of losing it if I changed jobs, and I was absolutely dependent on a weekly wage. Another cause for hesitation was a feeling that in accepting another offer I would be abandoning a 'sinking ship' and the people I had grown fond of. In 1939 Jonathan Cape himself asked me to come and see him if I wanted to change jobs, but with the outbreak of war I lost my Estonian passport and my permit and was not able to take up his offer. He reminded me of this when some years later, soon after the war, we met on the *Queen Elizabeth* on our way to the United States.

Six months after the outbreak of war, I married and Great Haseley, near Oxford, where Bernard had rented a house, gradually became my base. Bernard was serving in the Oxford and Bucks Light Infantry: he had joined up as soon as war was declared and had been posted to an Oxfordshire anti-aircraft battery. He was given forty-eight hours leave so that we could be married in London in May 1940.

Little did I then realise how long the war would last, or the changes it would bring. Unexpectedly, Bernard was to be the first member of our family to re-establish contact with Aunt Zoria and her children after the war had ended: they were in

Lübeck where Bernard, by then Lieutenant-Colonel, was able to locate them shortly after the German capitulation. But all of that was much later: I had long been married and by then had two children. At the outbreak of war, all we knew was that it would mean an abrupt end to the hectic existence we had led during the 1930s.

The beginning of the Second World War made life in London more orderly and purposeful for Moura. After I married, Molly Cliff proposed that she share her well-organised flat with Moura, and they lived together for many years until Molly's death. They were well looked after by an Italian cook-housekeeper. Gradually Moura's sitting-room began to bear the closest resemblance to a 'salon', while she herself was an inveterate party-goer. Many weekends were spent with me in Oxfordshire. But most important for Moura was the fact that she found regular work. After the collapse of the French armies in 1940 and the signature of an armistice with Germany by a new government under Marshal Pétain, the remnant of the French armed forces who wished to continue the fight against Germany came to England. There they accepted the leadership of Brigadier General de Gaulle, who had been Under-Secretary of State for War in the government of Paul Reynaud. There were, however, in London a number of intellectuals with political connections who did not automatically accept the political leadership of de Gaulle. Among these was an ambitious and highly clever journalist, André Labarthe, who started a monthly magazine in London called *La France Libre*. I believe it was Bruce Lockhart, who was then in the Ministry of Information, who introduced Moura to him.

The magazine was run by a lively editorial team including Raymond Aron, an economist of note who had already established a journalistic reputation in France; Madame Marthe Lecoutre, a left-wing French journalist; and her Polish husband, Stacho Shimonchek. For the launch of the magazine they badly needed the help of someone who had literary contacts in London and had a good knowledge of the French language and of France. Moura was well fitted to supply this need and soon became Jack-of-all-trades for the newly launched magazine. She helped Labarthe to raise funds from the Ministry of Information as well as from private supporters. She had sufficient literary contacts to be able to approach, on behalf of the magazine, distinguished writers such as George Bernard Shaw, H.G. Wells, and J.B. Priestley and persuade them to write for it. Very soon *La France Libre* came to be regarded in both British and French intellectual circles in London as the magazine which represented all that was best in the French literary tradition. Even Liddell Hart wrote to congratulate the magazine on its brilliant military articles and their insight and perceptive analysis of the German military campaign. These articles were not signed but were in fact written by Stacho Shimonchek, more often than not in my house in Oxfordshire.

Among the many generous supporters of *La France Libre* were Cecil and Marie-Alixe Michaelis, good friends of ours, who lived at Rycote Park near Thame in Oxfordshire and not very far from Great Haseley where I was now living with my small son, well away from the London Blitz. Marie-Alixe and Cecil knew many of the Free French leaders. While my husband was away in the army and my son was only a few months old, I was very happy to have the company of friends and 'refugees' from the London Blitz who wanted shelter and rest: between 1941 and 1944 the house was always full. Gradually I got to know all the members of the editorial staff of *La France Libre*, who were constantly on my doorstep asking for a few days' refuge. In the day they would write their articles for the next issue while I ran the house, grew vegetables, bottled fruit and administered to the demands of my baby son. In the evenings we played bridge, pooled our rations and cooked delicious meals with wartime rations. They were stimulating company. Marthe and Stacho became my close friends and were the most frequent visitors.

Sometimes Moura would bring H.G. Wells with her for the weekend. I had cleared a room for him, and occasionally he stayed with me for a whole week while Moura went back to London and returned the following Thursday or Friday. All morning he spent in his room writing. After lunch he would do

The Times crossword puzzle with incredible speed and then have a rest till tea-time. In the evenings he was extremely sociable and genial to everyone who happened to drop in, always firmly expressing his strong views, in particular on Catholicism, capitalism and the war. He enjoyed playing racing-demon and always teasingly accused Moura of cheating. Except for occasional visits to friends, Wells remained in London in his Hanover Terrace house. Throughout the war Moura continued to visit him every day. But his health had been declining for some time and though he was now being looked after by day- and night-nurses, he was getting weaker every day. On August 25th, 1946, he died peacefully at his house in London. He was seventy-nine. For Moura his death marked the end of an epoch and the loss of a dear friend.

3. Wells's drawing for Tania's son, John.

La France Libre had already folded up by that time. It was published in London until the end of the war, after which

André Labarthe and his team went back to France where they successfully launched a French magazine called *Constellation*, modelled on *Reader's Digest*.

Moura now needed a new interest. Shortly after H.G.'s death she went to see Alexander Korda, whom she had met with H.G. in 1934 when he was making a lavish film based on H.G. Wells's *The Shape of Things to Come*, a Utopian science fiction type of novel. Korda agreed to employ Moura as a reader, with her own little office, telephone and a secretary. She was paid only a small weekly wage but it gave her an entry into the film and theatre world. She had never worked regular hours before and found it difficult to get to the office on time. She devised a method by which she stayed in bed at home, having instructed her secretary to telephone at once if Korda or anyone else asked for her. The secretary was to tell the caller that Moura was out of the office 'at the moment' and ring her at once. She would then herself ring back the caller from her flat, as if from her office. If it was something easily dealt with on the telephone everything was all right; if, however, she was required to be in Korda's office, she would say that she just had to finish something in her own office and would be up shortly. She would then fling on some clothes, hail a taxi and in a few minutes be at Hyde Park Corner. Luckily it did not happen very often that anyone wanted her before midday, and luckily too the traffic then was not what it is today. I witnessed her do this on one or two occasions and was greatly amused.

Whether Korda knew all about it and shut an eye to her goings-on I don't know. I suspect that her role was primarily a civilising influence for his office. He enjoyed her company and they became close friends. Socially she was useful to him and she was often at his house in London for dinner, and sometimes accompanied him and his wife Alexa on their journeys abroad. When Korda died in 1956 Moura continued to act as historical adviser in a number of films, and even acted a small silent part in Carol Reed's film *The Accident*. She liked to be in the social and literary swim, to be busy in order to be in touch with people. Many of the best-known actors and writers appeared at her parties in Cromwell Road in those years.

She lived a long life on the fringe of literature, translating whatever she could persuade her publishing friends to give her. She was not a good translator. She spoke English, French and German well, but she did not 'possess' any of the languages as completely as a writer, or even a translator, should, if he or she is to be really successful. She would scribble away in longhand in bed, in a train, or even when she was in the company of people who did not really interest her. These scribbles were then passed to some devoted friend, who would complain and tease her but always ended up by correcting the English for her. Only then were the pages sent to be typed. The typist too complained but always ended up doing the job. Translations were very badly paid in those days, but Moura was grateful to be kept busy and accepted whatever publishers were haphazardly prepared to give her. The originals were often poor in themselves, but to her they were important. They also helped her to become a member in her own right of the PEN Club which she had been attending until then as friend of H.G. Wells. H.G. often scoffed at her translating-scribbles, but I have also seen him amiably and patiently sit and correct some of these same handwritten pages, and once he even got Aldous Huxley to write a preface to one of Moura's translations. Through her friend Nadia Benois, the painter, she was given the autobiography of Alexander Benois, the great choreographer of ballet, to translate. It was probably the most interesting and successful book out of some twenty titles that Moura translated, sometimes in collaboration with, or under the editorship of, a more professional writer – although somehow she managed to create the impression that the number of such books was considerably larger.

Some years after Stalin's death in 1958 Gorky's widow, Ekaterina Pavlovna, wrote Moura a charming, generous letter, telling her that she was now eighty years old, and suggesting that it would be nice to meet, as they had not seen each other since Gorky's death in 1936. Would Moura like to be invited to Moscow? The invitation was sent and a visa for ten days was obtained on the strength of it. Moura was overjoyed, even though she had a few misgivings before going. But after that there were many more short visits to the Soviet Union until her death in 1974. She stayed with the Gorky family, all of whom knew her well and were pleased to talk of old times, as by now they were attached to her almost as though she were a member of the family.

But finally, after Moura's eightieth birthday, she decided that to live in London without being able to continue her usual round of theatres, dinner parties or 'at homes' was not for her, and she made plans to leave London and move to Italy, where it would be warm and where she felt at home. My brother and his wife had already retired to a small house in Tuscany some years earlier, and before long a little country hotel suitable for retirement was found for Moura three miles from them. Here she was to have two rooms where she could house her belongings and enjoy the pleasures of life in Italy. Family and friends were to visit her as often as possible. None of us suspected when she left London that she had less than two months to live. I went out to her when she was taken ill, and remained in Italy for the last two weeks of her life. My brother and I were with her when she died on October 31st, 1974.

CHAPTER XIII

Moura

Many years ago, but when Moura was already in her fifties, I remember meeting Nico Henderson (now Sir Nicholas Henderson) at a party. He told me that he had, that day, been with three or four colleagues at what should have been a working lunch; but instead of discussing their subject, all four men had spent their lunch talking about Moura. None of them knew her at all well, though all of them were acquainted with her; and yet they all found that they shared a common fascination. Although they were unable to put their finger on what it was in her character that intrigued them, or to say what the cause of their fascination was, the very fact that she dominated their conversation testified to the power she could exert over people. It was not any great wisdom that she had imparted that set them talking, nor was it any particular incident that had pushed her suddenly into public prominence: it was simply the fact that, for the whole of her life, Moura was able to dominate and intrigue, to make herself the centre of people's lives, without them ever really knowing why it was.

That fascination has prompted many people to try to write my mother's biography; for here, they realised, was a great story covering some of the most interesting and turbulent years of this century, the story of a woman who had been in the midst of great events, and a story intriguingly ringed about with mysteries and tantalisingly unanswered questions. And yet the peculiar fact is that, despite several attempts, no biography has ever successfully been written, for it has never been possible to pin down the real truth behind the legends. Humphrey Trevelyan was once told by Moura that he was 'the only person I would entrust to write my biography'; yet even this was not true, as she said precisely the same to at least two other people. Sir Humphrey, however, found himself unable to write it, and told me, when I mentioned writing this book, that he had been forced to the conclusion that it was better to let the legend lie.

Another of those to whom Moura had entrusted the sole rights in her biography was Rache Lovat Dickson, the publisher and writer, who was in fact the only one who came anywhere near achieving it; and yet he too found that, the further he got into her story, the more elusive it became. There are no archives, and precious few letters; and my mother wrote almost nothing about herself. In interview she seldom actually revealed the truth about herself, and 'coming clean', after a lifetime of half-truths, was something she found almost pathologically impossible. In the end, Rache was forced to abandon his attempt: the story had to be more than that she had had such famous people as Wells and Gorky as her lovers, and yet it was impossible to get any further. What those who would write about her were left with was the intangible but powerful presence of one who, in Rache's words, was 'a survivor of a revolution who used her brains, her looks and the vitality of her nature, not only to survive but to enjoy the risky process'. In the end, together with George Robertson of the Canadian Broadcasting Corporation, Rache made a short documentary film about her which simply confirmed what people already knew, but which went nowhere towards explaining the mystery. It was Rache who later persuaded me to include in this book my own personal account of my mother.

Moura was determined not to be among those of her generation who were destroyed by war, revolution and the poverty of an emigré existence. She wanted a better life, to obtain which she was prepared to compromise and to flout all conventions. She set out to meet as many influential people as possible who might be of use to her. She also saw the advantage of surrounding herself with a legend. There was no one who was in a position to contradict the stories she told about herself. To most people in England, Russia was a strange and unknown world where anything could happen. Moura could allow her imagination to run wild, and people were intrigued by her stories. These were passed on from one friend to another and later appeared as gospel truth in various people's memoirs, making her all the more fascinating and more of a mystery. Shortly after her arrival and establishment in London, Bruce Lockhart's account of his mission to Russia fifteen years previously was published. English readers were much taken by the romantic aspect of the story, set against a fascinating political background, and were anxious to meet Moura in the flesh. All this helped to foster the aura of mystery about herself, which she was by no means in a hurry to dispel.

H.G. Wells, himself very much under the sway of that mystery, was told once by Aldous Huxley that this was a case 'where the story is greater than the individual'; and yet both have proved almost impossible to pin down. Those who would understand Moura are confronted and challenged with a paradoxical character full of deep divisions; with a story where rival versions conflict and the truth is elusive. Those who knew Moura testify at once to her courage, her charm, and her self-confidence: even her sharpest detractors do not deny her good humour, her warmth and her affection. And yet at the same time they also acknowledge the lack of scruple, the disregard for truth, the insatiable need of admiration and attention. She was somebody supremely attuned to the power of the impression she left: she behaved always according to the image she wanted people to have of her. She was an intelligent woman, without doubt; but was this really only native cunning and the ability to pick the brains of brilliant men and women without their realising it? My Aunt Assia, speaking of their childhood, once said, 'We were brought up to think of ourselves as demi-gods': how was it that somebody who had suffered as much, and lost as much, as my mother, could still expect and command such adulation? One way she achieved this, without doubt, was by exerting an emotional pull: she once told a friend of mine that she thought men would remain attached to her if she had slept with them. Yet the question remains of how much this was an egotistical desire to manipulate people, or a response to a deep need within herself. Certainly, once attached she never let go; and yet this seems to have been part of the attraction for those caught in this way.

If those paradoxes and questions have troubled her would-be biographers, then they have troubled me even more, for they have challenged something far more fundamental for me. And yet I feel that I must attempt some answer to these questions, for I alone am in a position to do so. The discovery of my mother is the discovery of my past, and represents my growing awareness of her, the problems which she faced and the solutions to them which she sought. It is a very personal story, for I write as one who was able to know the woman behind the legend. My mother spent much of her life presenting a front to the world and evading its questions; and yet the experiences that we had shared and gone through together gave us a unique closeness. We shared, if you like, a Russianness that we both held dear: I had loved Kallijärv, both for what it was and for what it increasingly came to represent for me in a world threatened by German Fascism, and, in all her travels, I recognised the same in my mother. I was interested to see that in his autobiography, Peter Ustinov remarks that Moura 'represented for me an indomitable side to the Russian character ... when I was in Moura's company, I felt deeply and serenely Russian'. We had shared that glorious summer in Sorrento, when I came closer to her and appreciated the deep bond of affection that existed between her and Gorky, which I came intuitively to understand, and their shared life (which later seemed to have little connection with the woman who held court in her apartment in the Cromwell Road).

My renewed relationship with Moura had started in the hardest possible way: when she returned to Kallijärv in 1921 she returned as a stranger, as one who had left her children and who had, as I later learned, been prepared to sacrifice them for ever. That I should come to love her says more for her character than her many passing attachments. Those she deceived most still loved and forgave her. In a curious way, I was both emotionally very close to her and at the same time aware of the emotional distance between us; I was always, I suppose, conscious that she had not been with us when I was growing up. This distance may have helped me later to be more objective about my mother than children usually are. And finally, living with her as an adult I was able to see the real woman who lived behind the public mask, on the rare occasions when it was allowed to slip; and it was in those very private moments that I really came to appreciate her stamina and her determination.

Recently, many allegations have been made about her, and I feel it is necessary to meet them as best I can, for in doing so I believe the roots of the enigma are exposed. They are roots that I myself came to find as I retraced my own story. Moura was somebody who could infuriate and deceive, who was capable of selfish and egotistical behaviour that was deeply wounding, particularly to those closest to her; I can testify that many times I found myself excluded, or even used, by her. I was, as I have said, dragged into her deceptions, used as an accomplice or an alibi, forced into telling lies for her, brought face to face on numerous occasions with the unscrupulous side of her character; but as I examine her story in the light of my own, the reasons for her behaviour become clearer. What also becomes clear is that she could not have been guilty of many of the things of which she was accused and which, never one pettily to distinguish between fame and notoriety, she was always reluctant to refute, preferring to let people think what they would, so long as she was at the centre of their thoughts.

The myths and legends that surround her make, of course, very good anecdotes; and one can well understand what it was, at the level of the 'good story', that kept Moura so endlessly reinventing her past, For anybody who wishes to come to terms with Moura's real story, it is necessary to discard much of the embellishment that now surrounds it. These are the anecdotes and snippets of her history that are to be found in all attempts to discuss her life; and they are there because she put them there. Everybody who knew Moura carried away with them a powerful sense of her personality, but this was at least partly fashioned by the aura of legend with which she herself surrounded it.

As with many good myths, they start even before she was born, and it is often not easy to distinguish fact from fiction.

She was proud of relating her family to an aristocratic, even Imperial, Russian past: not content with a father who was a respected lawyer, a senator and a landowner, she used to tell of great-aunts and grandfathers at the heart of Russian affairs, and most important, she could trace the Zakrevsky family back to Peter the Great, via his daughter Elizabeth and a morganatic marriage in 1742. To back this up, she used when younger to put on a false moustache: and the resemblance to Peter the Great was certainly striking. It is impossible to verify this story, and equally impossible to refute it, although it is certainly true that it was believed by some of her family, but there does not appear to be much circumstantial evidence to support it. But it is possible to refute the other stories about her early life.

There is one persistent rumour that she had come to England well before the outbreak of the First World War, and that she had studied at Newnham College in Cambridge. During this time she is supposed to have met my father who was a diplomat at the Russian Embassy in London. This is, of course, pure fantasy: she was never at Cambridge and my father was at the embassy in Berlin at the time. She also claimed to have been introduced to H.G. Wells by Maurice Baring as far back as 1914 at a party at the British Embassy. In his own book *Russia in the Shadows* Wells relates this story, but as he confesses in *H.G. Wells in Love*, it was Moura alone who remembered the meeting: he had no recollection of it. In fact, although Moura was back in St Petersburg in 1914, it is highly unlikely that this meeting took place; and one of the regrets she expressed to the end of her life was that she had not known Maurice Baring in Russia. What she wanted was an emotional hold over H.G., which she felt would be strengthened if she could also claim a long-standing fascination on her part.

She seems, in fact, to have been quite casual in telling people when she was born, for there were times when this could interfere with a good story. Thus she claimed to have been dining with Norman Douglas before the turn of the century at the British Embassy in St Petersburg when he apparently turned to her and asked her whether she had had syphilis.

Being only seventeen and not knowing what it was, but unwilling to appear naive, she replied that she could not remember, much to his confusion. A typical Moura story, showing herself the equal of any occasion; but of course impossible, not only because of chronology, but also because I remember the occasion at which she was told this story, which had actually happened to the sister of a close friend of ours, Bill Haslam, and I remember how surprised and delighted we all were when he first told it. When it came to anecdotes she was no respector of ownership – the perfect magpie.

Of course the events of the Russian Revolution create a romantic enough aura if you wish to interpret them in that way; but even here Moura embellished to cast a more heroic role for herself. She would tell the story that she had smuggled us children out of Petrograd and into Estonia, painting an even more lurid picture of what was already a very dramatic event: of course, she was in fact waiting behind in Petrograd with her sick mother, and it was Micky who took us. But she would also relate how she had crossed to Estonia on foot, and here again fact and fiction intermingle and give rise to all sorts of speculation. She used to maintain to some interviewers or friends that, when she realised how deeply in love with Bruce Lockhart she was, she decided to confront my father at Yendel, to tell him of the love affair, and to inform him she was leaving him. She then supposedly walked across the frontier to Estonia, met my father and told him this, and walked back to Petrograd. My father, distraught by what he had been told, remained at Yendel where he was later killed. Certainly my mother did go to Yendel, but it was not on foot, nor was it to tell my father about Lockhart: it was to be able to prove that my father could have made her pregnant, so that 'little Peter' would be legitimate. Perhaps the story of crossing to Estonia on foot is a relic of my father's ride from Reval to St Petersburg in a day; and one can see how she was unable to reveal the whole truth about her visit; but it clearly indicates the way she would recast her history.

Moura would also claim various different stories about her periods of imprisonment. As well as her arrest with Bruce

Lockhart, she would also claim to have been arrested, wrongly, for black market trading, and to have spent four months in prison after her abortive attempt to leave Russia in 1921. She spent, in fact, only a few days in prison on that occasion, and it is impossible to verify the other tale.

No one could dispute that she was an immensely courageous woman; the very fact of her survival in the circumstances she endured is sufficient testimony to that. There are other stories that illustrate her courage too; probably none more so than the scene described by Bruce Lockhart in *Memoirs of a British Agent* when he was being interrogated in his cell by Peters, the deputy head of the Cheka, with Moura also present. With a courage that extends well into folly she, having caught Bruce Lockhart's eye, slipped a note into one of his books and then, thinking that Lockhart had not seen, repeated the exercise even more ostentatiously, with the threat of discovery absolutely imminent. As has frequently been commented, in those days of desperation Moura displayed a fearlessness and an indomitable will to survive, by adapting wherever necessary and by compromising where she felt she had to.

She lived through stirring times and she was, without doubt, right at the heart of them: she had the gift of making herself welcome, and then apparently indispensable, in any of the circles within which she moved. Thus she was equally at home in the glittering world of the Imperial diplomatic society and in the group of Soviet revolutionary artists and writers; equally at ease in the committed milieu of Il Sorito and the hectic world of literary and social London of the 1930s. But she was also at pains to expand upon the idea of her own importance, and therefore stories abound of her confrontations with famous people. She would, for instance, tell of how she had been dancing the night away at a ball in the Yousoupov Palace while, in the room immediately below her, Rasputin was being murdered. Again, she would tell with relish of the occasion when she bearded Mussolini and took him to task for being suspicious of the radical changes that had overcome her character, turning an aristocrat into the companion of a socialist writer, by reminding him that he had himself once been the editor of a left-wing journal. It is impossible to get at the truth behind any of these incidents or anecdotes: almost certainly there is a basis of truth there, though well-hidden.

The most persistent, and the most damaging, rumours that have surrounded my mother relate to her alleged spying activities; and yet, when one examines them closely, one can see that all these stories, like the others, stem from my mother's compulsive need to reinvent the past, and exist in a world of half-truth and surmise, relating to an atmosphere rather than concrete certainties. In such an atmosphere, rumours of spying are bound to flourish, and they have continued to do so: most recently the case against her has been stated by Anthony West in his biography of his father, but his theory is based on accusations that have frequently been made before, and are constantly being repeated. These need now to be refuted, not only because of the pain they cause, but more important, because they distort the picture of my mother by ignoring the truly complex side of a character who felt the need to bolster herself with such fabrication.

Even the stories of her as a possible spy conflict head-on with each other; and all of them are shot through with the same sort of inconsistencies and inaccuracies that are to be found elsewhere. The stories seem to begin in 1916 when Moura is supposed to have been caught by the Germans spying for the Russian military authorities, and to have been sentenced to death. From this point on, it is alleged, she never once had any personal control over her actions, and was forced to act as instructed by her various masters. Needless to say, there is absolutely no evidence of her arrest in 1916: it is in fact impossible that she could ever have been anywhere near the German front. Quite apart from anything else, she was at the time living in Petrograd with her mother and two small children.

It is, however, the story of her involvement with the Cheka and its bearing on her relations with Bruce Lockhart, Gorky and Wells that have aroused the most notice. The reason for this, of course, is clear: there are several points in her life where the truth was deliberately concealed and speculation actively encouraged. In fact, the truth is far less exciting, if much more revealing.

One version of the story is that, after her arrest with Bruce Lockhart in 1918 following the attempt on Lenin's life, she was released by the Cheka on the condition that she would act as an informer, a role which she continued to perform, making no secret about it, throughout her relationship with both Gorky and Wells. But even before that, it has been suggested, she was already in the pay of the Russian secret services, and was being employed by them to spy on Bruce Lockhart himself. Thus we have yet another version of what happened when, in fact, she went to Estonia to give her unborn child a chance of legitimacy. The insinuations are that she either remained in Moscow, or went no further than Petrograd, but that in either case she was somehow getting in touch with, or reporting back to, her espionage masters. The letters to Bruce Lockhart, of course, prove this to be untrue, as well as testifying to the true emotional state of my mother during the affair, and to its long-lasting effect on her.

Less easily discounted, though equally false, is the allegation that Zinoviev, a member of the Politburo with special responsibility for Petrograd, granted Moura her freedom on condition that she would serve the secret police as an informer. Zinoviev had a fierce hatred of Gorky, and, as the story goes, used Moura to spy on him: thus her arrival at Kronverskaya Prospekt was the result of a carefully laid plan. Once there, however, the story continues that my mother was unable to prolong the pretence and confessed to Gorky the basis on which she had come to his apartment, and the mission she was intended to carry out. Gorky was supposed to have been so deeply impressed by her candour and honesty in this that, far from getting rid of her, he made himself her protector.

Then in the following year, 1920, Zinoviev is supposed to have arranged for her to spy on Wells during his visit to Petrograd. According to this story, the promoter of the idea of inviting Wells to Russia was Chicherin, then the senior diplomat in the Russian Ministry of Foreign Affairs. He persuaded Lenin to invite Wells on the grounds that Wells would be able to mobilise relief supplies for the Soviet Union in England and the United States; Chicherin then contacted Zinoviev, who suggested that my mother should be attached to H.G. throughout his visit to the Soviet Union.

When writing about this visit, Wells himself refers to Moura as having been 'assigned' to be his official guide and interpreter. The use of the word 'assigned' helps to reinforce West's theory that Moura was not acting of her own accord. The suggestion is also made that at the Cheka's request she accompanied Wells to Moscow to meet Lenin, though there is no evidence that she ever went to Moscow with Wells, and she always said that she had never met Lenin. Wells himself tells us that Zorin interpreted for him in Moscow.* The story of her being planted on Wells by the Cheka does not, unfortunately, take full account of the rather more prosaic facts. Chicherin, knowing that Gorky and Wells were old friends, had asked Gorky to invite Wells to stay in his large apartment on Kronverskaya Prospekt, and to look after him during his visit. Moura was the only member of Gorky's household, where she had been living for a year, who spoke fluent English. It was therefore natural that she should interpret for Wells and Gorky. There was no need to invent a 'controller' in the Cheka to assign her to this simple task.

It was natural that people were suspicious of her, and should cite discrepancies or half-truths as evidence of a secret life as a spy. In fact, the answer is far more basic and more human; owing to the insecurity of her own position, Moura felt the need constantly to play one man off against another. This explains the incident that sparked off the famous quarrel between Wells and Moura in 1934, when Wells, quite naturally, was hurt and outraged to find out from a member of Gorky's entourage in Moscow that Moura had in fact been there only a week beforehand, although she had always told him she could never return to Russia. In his recent biography, Anthony West would have us believe that

---

* *Russia in the Shadows*

Wells then confronted my mother, and that she frankly confessed to him 'the full extent of her involvement with the Russian secret services'. In his own autobiography, however, Wells makes no allusion to the possibility of Moura being a spy. He knew that Gorky was a powerful figure inside the Soviet Union after his return, and certainly realised that he was in a position to make arrangements for Moura to visit him in Russia. Wells's discovery that he had been persistently lied to by the woman he trusted caused him deep distress and revived his feelings of jealousy towards Gorky.

I was, in fact, present during H.G.'s visit that summer to Kallijärv, and clearly remember talking with him about the shock he had received on finding out about her duplicity. It is, I suspect, possible that Moura told him quite a story about her past. But the root of her behaviour is to be found in the need she felt then, and throughout her life, not to loosen her grip on anything or anybody, once she had got hold of them. She would employ any means, and seemed quite unscrupulous at times; most important, she would use what feminine wiles she had to maintain her hold over her lovers. She was afraid of jeopardising her relationship with H.G., for she knew that he had already been jealous of her previous connection with Gorky, but she was equally determined not to lose Gorky, her last link with Russia; and thus she contrived to keep up her relationship with both, and to outface any consequences. There was a brutal logic in what she told Wells that summer, which made him realise that a life shared with Moura was an illusion. Although she may have invented the episodes she hinted at, the impression she gave most strongly was that she was determined to be a survivor, and that she would never let anything get in the way of that; above all, she made it clear that she had to be taken on her own terms, and that she could never be dictated to. There was a determination and a fierceness in her behaviour towards Wells at that time which explain her survival far better than do the stories of spying.

Such stories, however, refuse to die, mostly because Moura herself refused to kill them. They are used as explanations for her ability to travel freely between Britain and Russia in the

1930s; and yet if she had in truth been a spy, she was such a blatant one that her movements would have been severely curtailed by her controller. Indeed, it is by no means clear for whom she was supposed to be spying, whether for the Russians or for British Intelligence. It seems poor cover for a Soviet agent to stand, as one critic has alleged, side by side with Stalin at Gorky's funeral.

Moura must have become quite used to the allegations of spying, for as early as her arrival in Estonia in 1921, she had been arraigned before the Court of Honour of the Baltic nobility, the *Ritterschaft*, to explain why she had stayed on in Russia; in her case suspicions must have been aroused by the fact that she had survived a revolution that had destroyed so many of her class and background, and had been able to remain in Soviet Russia. She had been able to dispel any suspicions at that time before an audience which was by no means sympathetic; but she clearly saw the attraction in allowing such stories about spying to circulate. It has also been claimed that, as late as 1940, she was employed by the Foreign Office in London to report on the activities of the Free French, by virtue of her position on the staff of the monthly review *La France Libre*; yet again, the story on examination proves to be quite without foundation, and simply, in fact, another attempt to come to terms with the enigma that my mother appeared to be.

However difficult it is actually to uncover it, the key to all my mother's behaviour, to all the stories and the deceptions, the rumours, but above all the charm and fascination, lies in her past. Like Micky, like Aunt Zoria, she was somebody who had lost everything and who had fought hard to rebuild her life. Events had conspired, at crucial points in her life, to expose her to exciting and bewildering new currents of thought and behaviour. The most crucial of these, I believe, was her meeting with Robert Bruce Lockhart who, at the very moment when the established world where she had been so secure and so dominant came crashing down around her, undermined her emotional security just as thoroughly. She had not known real love before, and now when she discovered it, it was all the more intense, bringing with it the promise of excitement and change. But having given herself so utterly, she found herself in the quite novel position of being rejected. Having opened herself completely to Bruce Lockhart, it must have been the cruellest of blows to her. Being the survivor that she was, she learned several lessons from it; above all, she learned never to give herself away again. From now on she would take what she could, but she would be careful what she gave. She knew that from now on she would have to fight for what she wanted.

As with so many survivors, she also had the instinct of hoarding to a very marked degree. This was particularly true of friends and acquaintances; all those who knew her remember the imperious nature of a summons from her, which could not be refused. But she was also a great hoarder of anecdote. In this she was again served well by events: the years immediately following the Russian Revolution were years of chaos, and it was impossible to confirm any of the stories that were told. It was, anyway, a period that gathered to itself images and myths that were already larger than life; and Moura, an opportunist, took advantage of people's already exaggerated imaginings of life in post-revolutionary Russia. It is also true that, apart from her letters, there is almost no documentary evidence about her. Again this has given rise to rumour and intrigue, appearing to illustrate the secretive nature of one wishing to avoid discovery, and even giving rise to the story of a fire, just before her death, in a caravan in Italy where all her papers had been taken. Unfortunately, the reality is less sensational: all her papers were destroyed by the new occupants of Kallijärv after the Second World War. But, as you would expect with one who played so consistently fast and loose with fact, she has herself become the victim of stories that not even she could have invented, such as the one that my father was hacked to death before her eyes in Estonia in 1917.

Her intelligence was intuitive rather than logical: the only time that I ever saw her at a loss for words was at a lunch party given by H.G. Wells where Rebecca West was another of the guests. Moura was unusually subdued and silent, and I realised then the cause of her discomfort. Rebecca West was a woman with a lively and, above all, disciplined intelligence. Moura was, I think, rather afraid of her, and uncomfortable in the presence of such a woman.

But she was herself a remarkable person, even for her remarkable times. As I came to know her better, I was myself frequently bewildered by the stories that I heard, and by the revelations that appeared and were not denied. I was, too, the victim of that possessiveness which, when we lived together in London before my marriage, made her encroach on my friendships while often keeping me at arm's length from her own friends, showing a jealousy that would occasionally make her secretive even about my existence. But I came to understand that fierce independence and to admire that strength of character, and the courage with which she had lived her life. And when all the myths and legends have been laid to rest, when all the many frustrations that she caused have been forgotten, it is on account of that strength of character and that refusal ever to give up, or ever to lose anything or anybody again, that one can say, despite what Aldous Huxley said, that the individual is in fact greater than the stories.

CHAPTER XIV

Postscript

When the war came, all our lives were changed; and so the war forms a natural conclusion to my story. But as my story is above all the story of Kallijärv, I should like it to end in the right place with my last visit in those troubled days of August 1939 just before war broke out.

I had as usual written to all my friends in Estonia, telling them that I was coming and when, and from their replies I knew that many of the people I loved would be there. But we had not invited friends from abroad to stay as the international situation was too uncertain.

Even before I arrived I was aware of one important difference between this visit to Kallijärv and any other I have ever made; it was my first visit since Micky's death. Micky had always been the focal point of my life in Kallijärv; she had lived for the visits of my mother and of us children. In the past the pleasure of my visits had been greatly increased by the bustle of shopping around to find presents for her from London, and by the joy of seeing her again and giving them to her. There was a great emptiness in our lives that summer.

Earlier that year when Micky was dying, we had been unable to get to her in Estonia, for we were all working in London; on the day that she died my mother and I hung on to the phone to Estonia and wept bitterly. I had been deeply affected by her death, for I had loved her as the person who had replaced my mother in my childhood. It now gave me some comfort to talk to Roosi, who had been with Micky to the end, and to know that Micky had not suffered for too long.

The absence of Micky coincided, I suppose, with a further loosening of Kallijärv's hold upon me. Although I could not help being full of memories of the past, I felt that for me it was now a time to look forward. I was twenty-four, an independent woman, and the matter that was uppermost in my mind that summer was marriage: how difficult I found it to make a decision. In any case, I was aware that I would never again be able to look on my childhood home in quite the same way.

I remember being met by our old friend Bengt Stackelberg when our boat arrived in Tallinn. We had lunch together in a favourite restaurant and inevitably found ourselves discussing the political situation. He wanted to know what people in England felt about the Munich agreement. I told him that most people by now felt that Neville Chamberlain had acted foolishly in being prepared to reach agreement with Hitler at any price; and I told him that many people felt ashamed and dismayed, recognising that, for all Hitler's promises, war was inevitable. But German propaganda had been highly successful in Estonia, and Bengt replied, quite genuinely, that he did not believe that Hitler really wanted war. I was shocked and upset to hear him say this.

From what he told me it seemed that the situation in Estonia was in many ways deceptively calm that summer. The Estonians appeared to be relatively unworried: recent internal political difficulties had disappeared and even the weather was particularly good. Although Hitler's invasion of Czechoslovakia in March and the seizure of the Lithuanian town of Memel had shown that small nations in Europe were not entirely safe, the Estonian Government appeared convinced that the existence of the three Baltic States between Germany and Russia was an effective guarantee. They believed that Hitler could not invade Estonia without precipitating a war with Russia, which he had no intention of doing in the summer of 1939, and that any aggression would be directed against England and France.

In Kallijärv the political discussions continued with our Baltic friends, many of whom believed passionately that Communism stood for all that was bad, and that any steps to prevent its spread, and even to ensure its eradication, would be justified. I remember in particular one Baltic friend, who had come over from a neighbouring estate for lunch, arguing that Hitler's only desire was to save the world from Communism, and that he had already done wonders in Germany. I could not agree with this, of course; but when this friend started trotting out all the Nazi arguments, and ended up claiming that Hitler was right to expel and victimise the Jews, because they had basically been responsible for the downfall of Germany, I could stand it no longer. I made it clear to him, as coldly as I could, that I felt it was time for him to leave, that there was no common ground between us, and that he would no longer be welcome at Kallijärv.

From incidents such as these I was brought face to face with the perniciousness of Nazi propaganda; but perhaps the most saddening thing I found on this last visit to Estonia was the extent to which it had permeated Baltic society. Everyone seemed to be finding excuses for Germany's behaviour, refusing to believe that it was leading the world to war. Aunt Zoria and Ricko Neff were the only ones who clearly saw that Hitler's was an evil nationalist régime determined to assert its mastery over others. Of those who visited us that summer, Ricko alone saw distinctly the threat of world war, and the need for England and France to make a stand against Hitler, although he feared it might already be too late.

Paradoxically enough, although we were surrounded with threats and rumours of war, Kallijärv itself seemed even more beautiful during that last summer. Despite all the arguments, I have the fondest recollections of my visit; it may be, of course, that memory plays tricks, but it seems to me that everything for which I cherished Kallijärv was more vivid. We swam in the lake with Uncle Sasha and the children; we walked in the woods with my cousins – above all we enjoyed the peace of those beautiful surroundings. I remember long talks with Aunt Zoria and also with Moussia Stackelberg, about my emotional entanglements in London and my indecision, hoping to clarify my own mind. Of course they couldn't really help me, for it was a decision I had to make for myself.

But for all its beauty, its peace and its calm, I knew that I would have to leave Kallijärv because, although I had looked upon my annual visit as a vitally important link with my past, and with all that I held dear, I wanted to be back in London: like so many young people of my generation, I felt most strongly a desire to take part in the great and terrifying events that, by the end of August 1939, I sensed were about to begin.

But I could feel that way only because I thought that Kallijärv would be safe, and would survive unchanged. It seems remarkable now, but it is true that when I left Kallijärv for England at the end of my visit, I had not even considered the possibility that I would never return, unless it were that I myself should be killed. To be sure, I thought it highly likely that it would be some years before I could come back, even that much might have changed in the world before that would be possible; but I did not entertain the thought that I might never see it again. Neither my mother nor I made any special arrangements for Kallijärv when we left that summer; and I suppose we felt that, having been the fixed point for us throughout such troubled and turbulent times, it was inconceivable that it would not remain a place of refuge for all of us in the years to come.

On September 1st, 1939 I caught the boat for Stockholm. I was not intending to return immediately to London: in fact, my plan was to spend a few days with a friend in Stockholm before catching the boat back to Tilbury. But while I was in Stockholm, Hitler invaded Poland, and my plans were completely altered. A summer that had been remarkable for me in the change that it promised, and in the memories that it had evoked, ended in the hustle and panic of a ship bound for London crammed with refugees fleeing the chaos that war would bring. The normal passenger complement of 200 had swelled to 2,000; and it was as we left Stockholm that I realised for the first time that I would probably never see Kallijärv again.

And that is my final picture: looking over the rail of a

crowded ship towards a country beyond the horizon which I could no longer see, a country which was about to lose its short-lived independence; but, above all, looking towards Kallijärv where I had spent my childhood, where I had learned so much that was valuable, and for the existence of which as our family home I shall always be truly grateful.

Index